瞬時に「わかる」！

数字の英語

Numbers in English

浅見ベートーベン

OpenGate

はじめに

学生としても、ビジネス・パーソンとしても、英語で数や金額などを伝えたり、聞き取ったりすることはとても大切です。特に、ビジネスの世界では、金額を聞き取れなかったり、間違って聞いたりすると、会社に大きな損害を与えることになりかねません。

一般的に日本人は英語で数を言ったり、聞き取ったりするのがとても苦手です。その理由は次のようにいくつか考えられます。

◎ 日常英会話では、数字について話す機会があまりないので、英語の数をどのように表現したらよいか、経験も知識も極端に少ない。
◎ 数学や科学を英語で習う機会がほとんどないので、数の表現を知らない。
◎ 数、序数、金額、幅、長さ、距離、電話番号などを正しい英語で学ぶ機会が学校ではほとんどない。
◎ 英語の先生たちが、数の言い方をマスターしていないので、教えることができない。

この本では、以上のような数を表現することができなかった理由を払拭して、これさえ押さえておけば、数を英語で伝えたり、聞き取ったりできるようになるという表現や問題を、テーマ別にたくさんご紹介しています。この本により、読者の皆様が、英語の数を怖がらず、自分からも発信し、相手の言っていることも聞き取れるようになることを、願っております。その結果、英語の成績が上がったり、ビジネスが成功裏に終わったりするようになれば、著者としてこんなにうれしいことはありません。

最後になりますが、編集の西村様には、本の全体像や問題の作成などで、とても大きな貢献をしていただきましたので、心から御礼いたします。

本書の使い方

本書では、英語での数の表現に慣れるために、たくさんの反復練習や問題を用意しています。

基本の構成は次のとおりです。

 表現紹介、反復練習

数字を一朝一夕にマスターすることはできません。何度も何度も練習することが大切です。

 書き取り問題

数字を正しく伝えるためにも、英語での読み方をきちんと身につけましょう。

 聞き取り問題

数字だけを読み上げた音声を聞き取れるようになりましょう。

 空欄埋め問題

文章や会話を聞いて空欄を埋めましょう。会話の中の数字を聞き取る練習になります。

CHAPTER 1 ▶ 基本の数字 ―基礎をマスターする―

まずは、基本からスタートです。初めは簡単な数字ですが、基本があやふやなままだと大きな数字には太刀打ちできません。しっかり基礎をマスターしましょう。

CHAPTER 2 ▶ 大きな数字 ―3桁区切りに慣れる―

日本語と英語の数字の大きな違いは、桁の区切りが違うことです。日本語では万、億、兆と4桁ずつ桁の呼び方が変わります。一方、英語ではmillion, billion, trillion とゼロ3つずつの区切りで、コンマごとに桁の呼

び方が変わります。

CHAPTER 2では、その英語ネイティブと同じ3桁区切りの感覚を身につけられるように、3パターンの反復練習に取り組みます。

反復練習1

視覚的にも3桁区切りの感覚を掴むために、「桁サポート」として桁の区切りごとに色を付けています。1つめのコンマはthousand、2つめのコンマはmillion…とパッと見ただけでもわかりやすくなっています。

反復練習2

3桁区切りの感覚に慣れたら、反復練習①とまったく同じ数字を「桁サポート」なしで読む練習をします。もし、うまくできなかったり難しく感じるときは、反復練習①に戻ってみましょう。

反復練習3

桁の感覚をしっかり掴んだら、どんな数字でも言えるように練習しましょう。

CHAPTER 3 ▶ 数字を使って伝える

基本の数字も大きな数字もマスターしたら、今度は「伝え方」を覚えましょう。

ビジネスシーンでも大切なお金や日付の言い方や、重さや長さを伝えるときの単位の呼び方など、11のテーマごとに多様な表現を紹介しています。

CHAPTER 3では、反復練習はありませんが、表現集として、数字を使って伝えるときのフレーズをいくつかピックアップしています。そのまま使ったり、語彙を入れ替えたりしながら、実際にどんどん使ってみてください。

CHAPTER 4 ▶ チャレンジ問題

CHAPTER 1からCHAPTER 3までユニットごとにいろいろな問題に取り組んできましたが、実際の会話やビジネスでは、どんな数字を伝えられるのかをあらかじめ予測するのは難しい場面もたくさんあります。CHAPTER 4では、どんな場面にも対応できる力をつけるために、ランダムな数字を使った問題を用意しました。CHAPTER 3までの反復練習や問題にくり返し取り組んだ後、ぜひ挑戦してみてください。

音声について

本書で紹介している数字の読み方、反復練習、表現集、聞き取り問題、空欄埋め問題の音声（英語）を、abceedアプリを使って聞くことができます。音声が収録されている箇所にはトラック番号を記載しています。

（画面イメージ）

① ページ下のQRコードまたはURLから、無料アプリ abceed（Android/iOS対応）をダウンロードしてください。

② 画面下の「見つける（虫メガネのアイコン）」タブをタップして、本書タイトルで検索します。表示された書影をタップし、音声の項目を選択すると、音声一覧画面へ遷移します。

③ 再生したいトラックを選択すると音声が再生できます。また、倍速再生など、学習に便利な機能がついています。

＊アプリの詳細は www.abceed.com にてご確認ください。

アプリのダウンロードはこちら

https://www.abceed.com/
abceedは株式会社Globeeの商品です。
アプリについてのお問い合わせ先
info@globeejp.com
（受付時間：平日の10時−18時）

CONTENTS

もくじ

CHAPTER

1

....

基本の数字

― 基礎をマスターする ―

▶ 1〜99

英語の数の数え方をご紹介します。

初めは基本的な数ですが、数が大きくなっても頻繁に使うものなので、つづりも発音も確実にマスターして身につけることが大切です。まずは基本から始めましょう。

🔄 反復練習

音声を聞き、声に出してくり返し練習しましょう。

まずは、1から9まで発音してください。　　　　　))) Track 001

1	one	**6**	six
2	two	**7**	seven
3	three	**8**	eight
4	four	**9**	nine
5	five		

次は、10から19まで発音してください。))) Track 002

10	ten		15	fifteen
11	eleven		16	sixteen
12	twelve		17	seventeen
13	thirteen		18	eighteen
14	fourteen		19	nineteen

次は、20から29まで発音してください。))) Track 003

20	twenty		25	twenty-five
21	twenty-one		26	twenty-six
22	twenty-two		27	twenty-seven
23	twenty-three		28	twenty-eight
24	twenty-four		29	twenty-nine

 21から99までは、10の桁の数字と1の桁の間に、「-」を付けます。

次は、30から39まで発音してください。))) Track 004

30	thirty	**35**	thirty-five
31	thirty-one	**36**	thirty-six
32	thirty-two	**37**	thirty-seven
33	thirty-three	**38**	thirty-eight
34	thirty-four	**39**	thirty-nine

thirty の th は、しっかりと舌を歯の間に挟んで発音してください。

次は、40から49まで発音してください。))) Track 005

40	forty	**45**	forty-five
41	forty-one	**46**	forty-six
42	forty-two	**47**	forty-seven
43	forty-three	**48**	forty-eight
44	forty-four	**49**	forty-nine

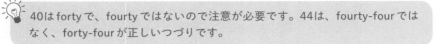

40は forty で、fourty ではないので注意が必要です。44は、fourty-four ではなく、forty-four が正しいつづりです。

次は、50から59まで発音してください。))) Track 006

50	fifty	55	fifty-five
51	fifty-one	56	fifty-six
52	fifty-two	57	fifty-seven
53	fifty-three	58	fifty-eight
54	fifty-four	59	fifty-nine

次は、60から69まで発音してください。))) Track 007

60	sixty	65	sixty-five
61	sixty-one	66	sixty-six
62	sixty-two	67	sixty-seven
63	sixty-three	68	sixty-eight
64	sixty-four	69	sixty-nine

次は、70から79まで発音してください。))) Track 008

70	seventy	**75**	seventy-five
71	seventy-one	**76**	seventy-six
72	seventy-two	**77**	seventy-seven
73	seventy-three	**78**	seventy-eight
74	seventy-four	**79**	seventy-nine

次は、80から89まで発音してください。))) Track 009

80	eighty	**85**	eighty-five
81	eighty-one	**86**	eighty-six
82	eighty-two	**87**	eighty-seven
83	eighty-three	**88**	eighty-eight
84	eighty-four	**89**	eighty-nine

最後は、90から99まで発音してください。))) Track 010

90	ninety	**95**	ninety-five
91	ninety-one	**96**	ninety-six
92	ninety-two	**97**	ninety-seven
93	ninety-three	**98**	ninety-eight
94	ninety-four	**99**	ninety-nine

いかがでしたか。うまく発音できなかった数は、くり返し練習してください。音声の発音に近づく事を目標に頑張ってください。焦ることはありません。確実に発音することが大切です。

次の数字の英語の発音を書きましょう。

1. 　11

2. 　29

3. 　38

4. 　52

5. 　89

6. 91

7. 14

8. 77

9. 45

10. 33

次の音声を聞き、その数字を書きましょう。　　))) Track 011

1.

2.

3.

4.

5.

6.

7.

8.

9.

10.

次の音声を聞き、空欄を埋めましょう。　　　))) **Track** 012

1.　A：What comes after [　　　]?

　　　B：[　　　].

2.　A：How many apples do you need?

　　　B：I need [　　　　　] apples.

3.　A：How can I help you?

　　　B：I would like to buy [　　　] black ballpoint pens
　　　　　and [　　　] red ballpoint pens.

4.　A：Are there enough copiers in each department?

　　　B：Each department has [　　　　　] copiers.

5.　A：We'll take [　　　] % off the list price.

　　　B：Thank you.

問題1 ▶ 書き取り

1. eleven
2. twenty-nine
3. thirty-eight
4. fifty-two
5. eighty-nine
6. ninety-one
7. fourteen
8. seventy-seven
9. forty-five
10. thirty-three

 問題2 ▶ 聞き取り

1. 18
2. 81
3. 93
4. 12
5. 59
6. 78
7. 30
8. 15
9. 67
10. 40

1. A：What comes after 41?

   B：42.

2. A：How many apples do you need?

   B：I need eight apples.

3. A：How can I help you?

   B：I would like to buy ten black ballpoint pens and five red ballpoint pens.

4. A：Are there enough copiers in each department?

   B：Each department has three copiers.

5. A：We'll take 15% off the list price.

   B：Thank you.

....

1. A：41の次には何が来ますか？

   B：42が来ます。

2. A：リンゴはいくつ必要ですか？

   B：リンゴが8個必要です。

3. A：何かお探しでしょうか？

   B：黒のボールペンを10本と赤のボールペンを5本買いたいです。

4. A：各部署に十分なコピー機がありますか？

   B：それぞれの部署がコピー機3台を所有しています。

5. A：定価から15％割引かせていただきます。

   B：ありがとうございます。

11と12は特別？

なぜ13からはteenがついて、11と12にはついていないのでしょうか。
13以上がthirteen、fourteen…となっているので、11ならone-teenで、
12ならばtwo-teenでいいのではないかと思われる方がたくさんいると
思います。英語の11と12はゲルマン語が語源で、elevenは10プラス1を
意味し、twelveは10プラス2を意味します。それと、12進法で、11と12
は13以上よりも頻繁に使うので、違った言い方がそのまま残ったという
説もあります。

ローマ数字でも11はXI、12はXII と書きます。Xは10を意味し、右側に
来るIは1を意味します。一方、左側に来ると、10からマイナスを意味し
ます。従ってIXは9となります。また、親指でその同じ手の他の4本の指
の関節を数えると12になります。指4本に関節が3つずつあるからです。
古代メソポタミアでは12進法が使われていたので、そのように数えてい
たそうです。

実は、12進法は現在の私たちの日常にも残っています。1年は12カ月、
時計は12が頂点ですね。はるか昔から、12が数の基準となっていたとい
うわけです。

02

▶100〜999

数字にもアメリカ英語とイギリス英語の違いがあります。100より大きい数字のとき、アメリカ英語ではandはつきませんが、イギリス英語では必ずandが入ります。

音声を聞いて読み方を確認しましょう。
（ ）はイギリス英語、（ ）の無いのはアメリカ英語です。))) Track 013

100	one hundred
101	one hundred (and) one
200	two hundred
212	two hundred (and) twelve
300	three hundred
345	three hundred (and) forty-five
400	four hundred
471	four hundred (and) seventy-one
500	five hundred
598	five hundred (and) ninety-eight

600	six hundred
634	six hundred (and) thirty-four
700	seven hundred
790	seven hundred (and) ninety
800	eight hundred
888	eight hundred (and) eighty-eight
900	nine hundred
999	nine hundred (and) ninety-nine

音声を聞き、声に出してくり返し練習しましょう。

100から900まで100単位で発音してください。 　))) Track 014

100	one hundred	**600**	six hundred
200	two hundred	**700**	seven hundred
300	three hundred	**800**	eight hundred
400	four hundred	**900**	nine hundred
500	five hundred		

次は、100から1ずつプラスして、発音してください。 　))) Track 015

100	one hundred	**106**	one hundred six
101	one hundred one	**107**	one hundred seven
102	one hundred two	**108**	one hundred eight
103	one hundred three	**109**	one hundred nine
104	one hundred four	**110**	one hundred ten
105	one hundred five		

次は、200から210まで発音してください。))) Track 016

200 two hundred	**206** two hundred six
201 two hundred one	**207** two hundred seven
202 two hundred two	**208** two hundred eight
203 two hundred three	**209** two hundred nine
204 two hundred four	**210** two hundred ten
205 two hundred five	

次は、300から310まで発音してください。))) Track 017

300 three hundred	**306** three hundred six
301 three hundred one	**307** three hundred seven
302 three hundred two	**308** three hundred eight
303 three hundred three	**309** three hundred nine
304 three hundred four	**310** three hundred ten
305 three hundred five	

次は、400から410まで発音してください。)))Track 018

400 four hundred

401 four hundred one

402 four hundred two

403 four hundred three

404 four hundred four

405 four hundred five

406 four hundred six

407 four hundred seven

408 four hundred eight

409 four hundred nine

410 four hundred ten

次は、500から510まで発音してください。)))Track 019

500 five hundred

501 five hundred one

502 five hundred two

503 five hundred three

504 five hundred four

505 five hundred five

506 five hundred six

507 five hundred seven

508 five hundred eight

509 five hundred nine

510 five hundred ten

次は、600から610まで発音してください。))) Track 020

600	six hundred	**606**	six hundred six
601	six hundred one	**607**	six hundred seven
602	six hundred two	**608**	six hundred eight
603	six hundred three	**609**	six hundred nine
604	six hundred four	**610**	six hundred ten
605	six hundred five		

次は、700から710まで発音してください。))) Track 021

700	seven hundred	**706**	seven hundred six
701	seven hundred one	**707**	seven hundred seven
702	seven hundred two	**708**	seven hundred eight
703	seven hundred three	**709**	seven hundred nine
704	seven hundred four	**710**	seven hundred ten
705	seven hundred five		

次は、800から810まで発音してください。))) Track 022

800	eight hundred	806	eight hundred six
801	eight hundred one	807	eight hundred seven
802	eight hundred two	808	eight hundred eight
803	eight hundred three	809	eight hundred nine
804	eight hundred four	810	eight hundred ten
805	eight hundred five		

次は、900から910まで発音してください。))) Track 023

900	nine hundred	906	nine hundred six
901	nine hundred one	907	nine hundred seven
902	nine hundred two	908	nine hundred eight
903	nine hundred three	909	nine hundred nine
904	nine hundred four	910	nine hundred ten
905	nine hundred five		

次は10単位で発音してください。

次は100から190まで発音してください。

100 one hundred	**150** one hundred fifty
110 one hundred ten	**160** one hundred sixty
120 one hundred twenty	**170** one hundred seventy
130 one hundred thirty	**180** one hundred eighty
140 one hundred forty	**190** one hundred ninety

次は、200から290まで発音してください。

200 two hundred	**250** two hundred fifty
210 two hundred ten	**260** two hundred sixty
220 two hundred twenty	**270** two hundred seventy
230 two hundred thirty	**280** two hundred eighty
240 two hundred forty	**290** two hundred ninety

次は、300から390まで発音してください。))) Track 026

300	three hundred	**350**	three hundred fifty
310	three hundred ten	**360**	three hundred sixty
320	three hundred twenty	**370**	three hundred seventy
330	three hundred thirty	**380**	three hundred eighty
340	three hundred forty	**390**	three hundred ninety

次は、400から490まで発音してください。))) Track 027

400	four hundred	**450**	four hundred fifty
410	four hundred ten	**460**	four hundred sixty
420	four hundred twenty	**470**	four hundred seventy
430	four hundred thirty	**480**	four hundred eighty
440	four hundred forty	**490**	four hundred ninety

次は、500から590まで発音してください。))) Track 028

500	five hundred	**550**	five hundred fifty
510	five hundred ten	**560**	five hundred sixty
520	five hundred twenty	**570**	five hundred seventy
530	five hundred thirty	**580**	five hundred eighty
540	five hundred forty	**590**	five hundred ninety

次は、600から690まで発音してください。))) Track 029

600	six hundred	**650**	six hundred fifty
610	six hundred ten	**660**	six hundred sixty
620	six hundred twenty	**670**	six hundred seventy
630	six hundred thirty	**680**	six hundred eighty
640	six hundred forty	**690**	six hundred ninety

次は、700から790まで発音してください。

))) Track 030

700 seven hundred	**750** seven hundred fifty
710 seven hundred ten	**760** seven hundred sixty
720 seven hundred twenty	**770** seven hundred seventy
730 seven hundred thirty	**780** seven hundred eighty
740 seven hundred forty	**790** seven hundred ninety

次は、800から890まで発音してください。

))) Track 031

800 eight hundred	**850** eight hundred fifty
810 eight hundred ten	**860** eight hundred sixty
820 eight hundred twenty	**870** eight hundred seventy
830 eight hundred thirty	**880** eight hundred eighty
840 eight hundred forty	**890** eight hundred ninety

CHAPTER 1 ▼ 基本の数字 ──基礎をマスターする──

最後は、900から990まで発音してください。))) Track 032

900	nine hundred	**950**	nine hundred fifty
910	nine hundred ten	**960**	nine hundred sixty
920	nine hundred twenty	**970**	nine hundred seventy
930	nine hundred thirty	**980**	nine hundred eighty
940	nine hundred forty	**990**	nine hundred ninety

いかがでしたか。うまく発音できなかった数は、くり返し練習してください。音声の発音に近づく事を目標に頑張ってください。焦ることはありません。確実に発音することが大切です。

問題1 ▶ 書き取り

解答は43ページ

次の数字の英語の発音を書きましょう。

米国式と英国式で書いてみましょう。英国式はかっこでくくってください。

1. 210

2. 530

3. 698

4. 451

5. 123

CHAPTER 1 ▼ 基本の数字 ── 基礎をマスターする ──

6. 733

7. 888

8. 911

9. 341

10. 213

次の音声を聞き、その数字を書きましょう。　　))) Track 033

1.

2.

3.

4.

5.

6.

7.

8.

9.

10.

次の音声を聞き、空欄を埋めましょう。　　　　))) **Track** 034

1.
A：How many books do you have?

B：I have [　　　　] books.

2.
A：How many countries are in the United Nations?

B：[　　　　] countries.

3.
A：How long is this film?

B：Running time is [　　　　] minutes.

4.
A：There are over [　　　　] different varieties of cherry trees.

B：Really? I didn't know that.

5.
A：How many friends do you have on Facebook?

B：I have [　　　　] friends.

問題 1 ▶ 書き取り

1. two hundred (and) ten
2. five hundred (and) thirty
3. six hundred (and) ninety-eight
4. four hundred (and) fifty-one
5. one hundred (and) twenty-three
6. seven hundred (and) thirty-three
7. eight hundred (and) eighty-eight
8. nine hundred (and) eleven
9. three hundred (and) forty-one
10. two hundred (and) thirteen

 問題 2 ▶ 聞き取り

1. 198
2. 350
3. 896
4. 542
5. 232
6. 337
7. 777
8. 931
9. 413
10. 614

1. A：How many books do you have?

   B：I have 260 books.

2. A：How many countries are in the United Nations?

   B：193 countries.

3. A：How long is this film?

   B：Running time is 125 minutes.

4. A：There are over 600 different varieties of cherry trees.

   B：Really? I didn't know that.

5. A：How many friends do you have on Facebook?

   B：I have 580 friends.

1. A：本を何冊持っていますか？

   B：260冊持っています。

2. A：国連に加盟しているのは何カ国ですか？

   B：193カ国です。

3. A：この映画はどれくらいの長さですか？

   B：上映時間は125分です。

4. A：桜の木は600種類以上あるんですよ。

   B：本当に？知りませんでした。

5. A：Facebookで何人の友達がいますか？

   B：580人の友達がいます。

Coffee Break

指を使った数え方：日本式と欧米式

ものを数えるとき、日本式では、1から5までは右手の親指を折り、6か
らは左手の親指を折って、10まで数えます。一方欧米式では、手のひら
を内側にして握った状態から右手の親指を開き、順番に人差し指から小
指まで数え、次に、左手の小指を開いて、最後に親指を開いて10まで数
えます。日本式では指を折り、欧米式では指を開く、という違いがあり
ます。

▶ 序数

序数はものの順番を表す数で、first 1番目、second 2番目、third 3番目のように使われます。1番目から9番目までは英語で書き、10番目からは数字で書きます。

例：first, second, third, fourth, fifth, sixth, seventh, eighth, ninth, 10th, 11th, 12thのようにつづります。

🔄 反復練習

音声を聞き、声に出してくり返し練習しましょう。

1番目から99番目まで　　　　　　　　　　　　　　　　))) Track 035

first	sixth
second	seventh
third	eighth
fourth	ninth
fifth	

10th	tenth	**15th**	fifteenth
11th	eleventh	**16th**	sixteenth
12th	twelfth	**17th**	seventeenth
13th	thirteenth	**18th**	eighteenth
14th	fourteenth	**19th**	nineteenth

20th	twentieth	**25th**	twenty-fifth
21st	twenty-first	**26th**	twenty-sixth
22nd	twenty-second	**27th**	twenty-seventh
23rd	twenty-third	**28th**	twenty-eighth
24th	twenty-fourth	**29th**	twenty-ninth

30th	thirtieth		**35th**	thirty-fifth
31st	thirty-first		**36th**	thirty-sixth
32nd	thirty-second		**37th**	thirty-seventh
33rd	thirty-third		**38th**	thirty-eighth
34th	thirty-fourth		**39th**	thirty-ninth

40th	fortieth		**45th**	forty-fifth
41st	forty-first		**46th**	forty-sixth
42nd	forty-second		**47th**	forty-seventh
43rd	forty-third		**48th**	forty-eighth
44th	forty-fourth		**49th**	forty-ninth

CHAPTER 1 ▼ 基本の数字 —基礎をマスターする—

50th	fiftieth
51st	fifty-first
52nd	fifty-second
53rd	fifty-third
54th	fifty-fourth

55th	fifty-fifth
56th	fifty-sixth
57th	fifty-seventh
58th	fifty-eighth
59th	fifty-ninth

60th	sixtieth
61st	sixty-first
62nd	sixty-second
63rd	sixty-third
64th	sixty-fourth

65th	sixty-fifth
66th	sixty-sixth
67th	sixty-seventh
68th	sixty-eighth
69th	sixty-ninth

70th	seventieth	**75th**	seventy-fifth
71st	seventy-first	**76th**	seventy-sixth
72nd	seventy-second	**77th**	seventy-seventh
73rd	seventy-third	**78th**	seventy-eighth
74th	seventy-fourth	**79th**	seventy-ninth

80th	eightieth	**85th**	eighty-fifth
81st	eighty-first	**86th**	eighty-sixth
82nd	eighty-second	**87th**	eighty-seventh
83rd	eighty-third	**88th**	eighty-eighth
84th	eighty-fourth	**89th**	eighty-ninth

90th	ninetieth	**95th**	ninety-fifth
91st	ninety-first	**96th**	ninety-sixth
92nd	ninety-second	**97th**	ninety-seventh
93rd	ninety-third	**98th**	ninety-eighth
94th	ninety-fourth	**99th**	ninety-ninth

100番目から1,000番目まで

100th	one-hundredth	**600th**	six-hundredth
200th	two-hundredth	**700th**	seven-hundredth
300th	three-hundredth	**800th**	eight-hundredth
400th	four-hundredth	**900th**	nine-hundredth
500th	five-hundredth	**1,000th**	one-thousandth

次の数字の英語の発音を書きましょう。

1. 17th

2. 43rd

3. 68th

4. 59th

5. 1,000th

次の音声を聞き、その数字を書きましょう。　　))) Track 046

1.

2.

3.

4.

5.

次の音声を聞き、空欄を埋めましょう。   ))) **Track** 047

1. September is the [   ] month in the year.

2. Our apartment is on the [   ] floor.

3. This is the [   ] CD the band has released.

4. Jack came in [   ] and was awarded the bronze medal.

5. Witnessing a traffic accident, the doctor provided [   ] aid.

6. A：Are you the [   ] candidate in the list?
B：No, I'm the [   ] candidate.

7.
A : Would you repeat your question?

B : This is the [   ] time that I'm repeating my question.

8.
A : What is your company's national sales ranking?

B : Our company ranks [   ] in the nation.

9.
A : How did your team do?

B : We took [   ] place.

10.
A : What anniversary is this?

B : It's the [   ] anniversary of our corporation.

問題1 ▶ 書き取り

1. seventeenth
2. forty-third
3. sixty-eighth
4. fifty-ninth
5. one-thousandth

問題2 ▶ 聞き取り

1. 25th
2. 72nd
3. 100th
4. 86th
5. 31st

問題3 ▶ 空欄埋め

1. September is the ninth month in the year.
2. Our apartment is on the 26th floor.
3. This is the 32nd CD the band has released.
4. Jack came in third and was awarded the bronze medal.
5. Witnessing a traffic accident, the doctor provided first aid.
6. A：Are you the fifth candidate in the list?
   B：No, I'm the sixth candidate.
7. A：Would you repeat your question?

B：This is the third time that I'm repeating my question.

8. A：What is your company's national sales ranking?

   B：Our company ranks twenty-third in the nation.

9. A：How did your team do?

   B：We took second place.

10. A：What anniversary is this?

    B：It's the 100th anniversary of our corporation.

....

1. 9月は、1年の内、9番目の月です。

2. 私たちのアパートは、26階にあります。

3. これは、そのバンドがリリースした32枚目のCDです。

4. ジャックは3位になり、銅メダルを授与されました。

5. その交通事故を目撃して、その医師は応急手当（最初の手当て）を施した。

6. A：あなたはリストにのっている5番目の候補者ですか？

   B：いいえ、6番目の候補者です。

7. A：あなたの質問をくり返していただけませんか。

   B：質問をくり返すのはこれが3度目ですよ。

8. A：御社は、国内営業で何番目のランクですか。

   B：我が社は、国内で23番目に位置します。

9. A：あなたのチームはどうでしたか？

   B：2位になりました。

10. A：これは何のアニバーサリーですか？

    B：我が社の100周年記念です。

英語で「何番目」は何という？

. . . .

日本語と違い、英語には「何番目」と言う言葉がありません。従って、「トランプ大統領は、米国の何番目の大統領ですか?」と尋ねるのが、とても大変です。

もし、英語にhow mannyeth president「何番目の大統領」という言葉があれば、簡単にHow mannyeth president is Donald Trump? と言えるのですが、こんな英語が日常使われることはありません。それでは、どんな表現をすればいいのでしょうか?次のような表現を使わざるを得ません。

1. **How many presidents were there before President Trump?**
   トランプ大統領の前に何人の大統領がいましたか?

2. **A：How many Presidents of the United States have there been before the current President Trump?**
   B：There were 44 presidents before him.
   A：現在のトランプ大統領の前に何人のアメリカ大統領がいましたか?
   B：彼の前には44人の大統領がいました。

3. **A：How many presidents preceded Donald Trump?**
   B：Forty-four.
   A：ドナルド・トランプの前には何人の大統領がいましたか?
   B：44人です。

4. **A：Where is Trump in the sequential order of U.S. presidents?**
   B：Donald Trump is the 45th President of the U.S.A.
   A：アメリカ大統領としてトランプは時系列で何番ですか?
   B：ドナルド・トランプはアメリカ合衆国の45番目の大統領です。

5. **Where is Trump in the order of U.S. presidents?**

アメリカ大統領の順番で、トランプは何番ですか？

6. **What place does Trump hold in the sequence of presidents?**

トランプ大統領は順序数詞で何番ですか？

7. **Where does Donald Trump fall in the sequence of US presidents?**

ドナルド・トランプはアメリカ大統領の順番でどこに位置しますか？

さて、一番適切な表現はどれでしょうか？

第1番目と第2番目がかなり良い表現です。しかし、それでも、答えは何番目ではなく、何番になってしまいます。次にあげる二つの表現のどちらかが、一番適切ではないでしょうか。

A：What number is President Trump?
B：He is number 45.

A：トランプ大統領は何番でしょうか？
B：彼は45番です。

A：What number president is Trump?
B：He is the 45th president.

A：トランプ大統領は何番でしょうか？
B：彼は45番目の大統領です。

この話を読み終わって、英語で「何番目」と言うのがいかに難しいか、おわかりになったのではないでしょうか。

04

▶ 正負の数、分数、小数

正の数　　　　　　　　　　　　　　　)))Track 048

+5	plus five
+6.2	plus six point two
+15.7	plus fifteen point seven

負の数　　　　　　　　　　　　　　　)))Track 049

-8	minus eight
-12.4	minus twelve point four
-75.242	minus seventy-five point two four two
+or-5	plus or minus five

分数

英語で分数は fractions、分子は numerator、分母は denominator といいます。3/8の場合、3が numerator で8が denominator です。))) **Track 050**

1/2	a half, one-half, one over two
2分の1マイル	a half mile/half a mile
1.5キログラム	one and a half kilograms, one point five kilograms

💡 2キログラムから複数になるのではなく、1キログラムを少しでも超えれば、複数の kilograms になるのを覚えておいてください。

1/3	a third/one-third, one over three
3分の1ポンド	a third of a pound, one-third of a pound
2/3	two-thirds, two over three

💡 one-third では、third の後ろに s はつきませんが、two-thirds では s がつきます。one-third がふたつあるので複数形になるのです。

1/4	a quarter/one-quarter, a fourth, one-fourth
3/4	three-quarters, three-fourths, three over four

 💡 1/4ポンドの重さのハンバーグは a quarter pounder と呼びます。

1/5	a fifth, one-fifth, one over five
3/5	three-fifths, three over five
1/10	one-tenth, one over ten
4/10	four-tenths, four over ten
13/18	thirteen-eighteenths, thirteen over eighteen
24/26	twenty-four twenty-sixths, twenty-four over twenty-six
1/100	a hundredth, (one) one-hundredth, one over one hundred
5/100	five (one-) hundredths, five over one hundred
43/100	forty-three (one-) hundredths, forty-three over one hundred
27/152	twenty-seven one hundred fifty-seconds, twenty-seven over one hundred fifty-two

123/678	one hundred twenty-three six hundred seventy-eighths, one hundred twenty-three over six hundred seventy-eight
234/567	two hundred thirty-four five hundred sixty-sevenths, two hundred thirty-four over five hundred sixty-seven
1/1000	a thousand, (one) one-thousandth
1時間の4分の3 (すなわち45分間)	three quarters of an hour

About a quarter of the people in this city are non-residents.

この都市にいる4分の1は居住していない人たちです。

帯分数

1 1/2	one and a half
1 3/5	one and three-fifths
3 1/2	three and a half
8 7/8	eight and seven-eighths/eight and seven over eight

小数

英語で小数は decimals といいます。

小数点	a decimal point
0.1	(zero) point one, ten percent
0.5	(zero) point five, fifty percent
0.15	(zero) point one five, fifteen percent
0.33	(zero) point three three, thirty-three percent
0.01	(zero) point zero one, one (one-) hundredth, one percent
0.000312	(zero) point zero zero zero three one two

6.04	six point zero four
8.716	eight point seven one six
0.7 グラム	(zero) point seven grams
1.119 メーター	one point one one nine meters
15.8 オンス	fifteen point eight ounces

> 1 pound は16 ounces です。10 ounces ではないので、注意してください。ちなみに1 foot は、10 inches ではなく12 inches に相当します。

12.5 ポンド	twelve and a half pounds, twelve point five pounds

次の数字の英語の発音を書きましょう。
二通りの読み方がある場合には、両方書いてください。

1.　3/8

2.　6/7

3.　1/500

4.　1 1/3

5.　12 3/100

6.　0.123

7.　20.2020

次の音声を聞き、その数字を書きましょう。　　　　)))Track 053

....

1.

....

2.

....

3.

....

4.

....

5.

....

6.

....

7.

....

8.

....

次の音声を聞き、空欄を埋めましょう。　　))) Track 054

1. One meter is [　　　　　　　　　　] of one kilometer.

2. [　　　　　　　　　　] of our employees are college graduates.

3. Only [　　　　　　] of wives living in this area have jobs.

4. [　　　　　　　] of developers in this laboratory have master's degrees.

5. [　　　　　　　　　　　　] centimeters equals 12 inches.

▶ 解答・日本語訳

問題 1 ▶ 書き取り

1. three-eighths, three over eight
2. six-sevenths, six over seven
3. one/a five-hundredth
4. one and one-third
5. twelve and three (one-) hundredths
6. (zero) point one two three
7. twenty point two zero two zero

問題 2 ▶ 聞き取り

1. 5/8
2. 3/100
3. 234/567
4. 2 3/4
5. 7 7/8
6. 3.1001
7. 0.001
8. 90.00211

1. One meter is one-thousandth of one kilometer. (1/1000)
2. Three-fourths of our employees are college graduates. (3/4)
3. Only one-fifth of wives living in this area have jobs. (1/5)
4. Four-fifths of developers in this laboratory have master's degrees. (4/5)
5. Thirty point four eight centimeters equals 12 inches. (30.48)

1. 1メートルは1キロメートルの1000分の1です。
2. 弊社社員の3/4は大卒です。
3. この地域の住民の妻は1/5しか働いていません。
4. この研究所の開発者の4/5は修士号を持っています。
5. 30.48cm は12インチです。

CHAPTER

2

· ·

大きな数字

—3桁区切りに慣れる—

01 ▶ thousand

日本人は、大きい数字になると千の単位よりも、万の単位で考えることが多いものです。一方で欧米人は、ゼロの数が4つ以上の場合、後ろからゼロが3つあるとその前にコンマを置いて区切って読みます。

例：1,000、10,000、100,000

つまり、英語には万の位の呼び方はありません。千の位の前をひとまとめにして呼びます。彼らのこの読み方のルールをしっかりと理解し、自分もそのように読む癖をつけることが、英語の数字感覚を身につけるポイントになります。例えば、10,000は1万ではなく、千が10でten thousandと読みます。100,000は10万ではなく、千が100あるのでone hundred thousandと読みます。

800,000は80万ではなく、千が800あるのでeight hundred thousandと読みます。120,000はone hundred twenty thousandとなります。

音声を聞いて読み方を確認しましょう。

（and）はイギリスの読み方で、（ ）がないのがアメリカの読み方です。

1,001	one thousand (and) one
1,101	one thousand one hundred (and) one
2,001	two thousand (and) one
2,101	two thousand one hundred (and) one

two thousand のあとにsがついて two thousands にならないことを覚えてください。

3,001	three thousand (and) one
3,101	three thousand one hundred (and) one
4,001	four thousand (and) one
4,101	four thousand one hundred (and) one
5,001	five thousand (and) one
5,101	five thousand one hundred (and) one
6,001	six thousand (and) one
6,101	six thousand one hundred (and) one
7,001	seven thousand (and) one

7,101	seven thousand one hundred (and) one
8,001	eight thousand (and) one
8,101	eight thousand one hundred (and) one
9,001	nine thousand (and) one
9,101	nine thousand one hundred (and) one

))) Track 056

10,000	ten thousand
20,000	twenty thousand
30,000	thirty thousand
40,000	forty thousand
50,000	fifty thousand
60,000	sixty thousand
70,000	seventy thousand
80,000	eighty thousand
90,000	ninety thousand

100,000	one hundred thousand
200,000	two hundred thousand
300,000	three hundred thousand
400,000	four hundred thousand
500,000	five hundred thousand
600,000	six hundred thousand
700,000	seven hundred thousand
800,000	eight hundred thousand
900,000	nine hundred thousand

音声を聞き、声に出してくり返し練習しましょう。

1,000
thousand

10,000
thousand

100,000
thousand

2,340
thousand

56,000
thousand

789,000
thousand

CHAPTER 2 ▼ 大きな数字 ──3桁区切りに慣れる──

one thousand

ten thousand

one hundred thousand

two thousand three hundred (and) forty

fifty-six thousand

seven hundred eighty-nine thousand

音声を聞き、声に出してくり返し練習しましょう。

CHAPTER 2 ▼ 大きな数字 ──3桁区切りに慣れる──

1,000

10,000

100,000

2,340

56,000

789,000

one thousand

ten thousand

one hundred thousand

two thousand three hundred (and) forty

fifty-six thousand

seven hundred eighty-nine thousand

反復練習 3 ▶ もっと練習

音声を聞き、声に出してくり返し練習しましょう。　))) **Track** 060

1,000	one thousand/ten hundred
1,100	one thousand one hundred/eleven hundred
1,200	one thousand two hundred/twelve hundred
1,300	one thousand three hundred/thirteen hundred
1,400	one thousand four hundred/fourteen hundred
1,500	one thousand five hundred/fifteen hundred
1,600	one thousand six hundred/sixteen hundred
1,700	one thousand seven hundred/seventeen hundred
1,800	one thousand eight hundred/eighteen hundred
1,900	one thousand nine hundred/nineteen hundred

))) **Track** 061

2,000	two thousand/twenty hundred
2,100	two thousand one hundred/twenty-one hundred

CHAPTER 2 ▼ 大きな数字 —3桁区切りに慣れる—

2,200 two thousand two hundred/twenty-two hundred

2,300 two thousand three hundred/twenty-three hundred

2,400 two thousand four hundred/twenty-four hundred

2,500 two thousand five hundred/twenty-five hundred

2,600 two thousand six hundred/twenty-six hundred

2,700 two thousand seven hundred/twenty-seven hundred

2,800 two thousand eight hundred/twenty-eight hundred

2,900 two thousand nine hundred/twenty-nine hundred

))) Track 062

3,000 three thousand/thirty hundred

3,100 three thousand one hundred/thirty-one hundred

3,200 three thousand two hundred/thirty-two hundred

3,300 three thousand three hundred/thirty-three hundred

3,400 three thousand four hundred/thirty-four hundred

3,500 three thousand five hundred/thirty-five hundred

3,600 three thousand six hundred/thirty-six hundred

3,700 three thousand seven hundred/thirty-seven hundred

3,800 three thousand eight hundred/thirty-eight hundred

3,900 three thousand nine hundred/thirty-nine hundred

))) Track 063

4,000 four thousand/forty hundred

4,100 four thousand one hundred/forty-one hundred

4,200 four thousand two hundred/forty-two hundred

4,300 four thousand three hundred/forty-three hundred

4,400 four thousand four hundred/forty-four hundred

4,500 four thousand five hundred/forty-five hundred

4,600 four thousand six hundred/forty-six hundred

4,700 four thousand seven hundred/forty-seven hundred

4,800 four thousand eight hundred/forty-eight hundred

4,900 four thousand nine hundred/forty-nine hundred

5,000   five thousand/fifty hundred

5,100   five thousand one hundred/fifty-one hundred

5,200   five thousand two hundred/fifty-two hundred

5,300   five thousand three hundred/fifty-three hundred

5,400   five thousand four hundred/fifty-four hundred

5,500   five thousand five hundred/fifty-five hundred

5,600   five thousand six hundred/fifty-six hundred

5,700   five thousand seven hundred/fifty-seven hundred

5,800   five thousand eight hundred/fifty-eight hundred

5,900   five thousand nine hundred/fifty-nine hundred

6,000   six thousand/sixty hundred

6,100   six thousand one hundred/sixty-one hundred

6,200   six thousand two hundred/sixty-two hundred

6,300   six thousand three hundred/sixty-three hundred

6,400	six thousand four hundred/sixty-four hundred
6,500	six thousand five hundred/sixty-five hundred
6,600	six thousand six hundred/sixty-six hundred
6,700	six thousand seven hundred/sixty-seven hundred
6,800	six thousand eight hundred/sixty-eight hundred
6,900	six thousand nine hundred/sixty-nine hundred

))) Track 066

7,000	seven thousand/seventy hundred
7,100	seven thousand one hundred/seventy-one hundred
7,200	seven thousand two hundred/seventy-two hundred
7,300	seven thousand three hundred/seventy-three hundred
7,400	seven thousand four hundred/seventy-four hundred
7,500	seven thousand five hundred/seventy-five hundred
7,600	seven thousand six hundred/seventy-six hundred

7,700	seven thousand seven hundred/seventy-seven hundred
7,800	seven thousand eight hundred/seventy-eight hundred
7,900	seven thousand nine hundred/seventy-nine hundred

))) Track 067

8,000	eight thousand/eighty hundred
8,100	eight thousand one hundred/eighty-one hundred
8,200	eight thousand two hundred/eighty-two hundred
8,300	eight thousand three hundred/eighty-three hundred
8,400	eight thousand four hundred/eighty-four hundred
8,500	eight thousand five hundred/eighty-five hundred
8,600	eight thousand six hundred/eighty-six hundred
8,700	eight thousand seven hundred/eighty-seven hundred
8,800	eight thousand eight hundred/eighty-eight hundred
8,900	eight thousand nine hundred/eighty-nine hundred

9,000	nine thousand/ninety hundred
9,100	nine thousand one hundred/ninety-one hundred
9,200	nine thousand two hundred/ninety-two hundred
9,300	nine thousand three hundred/ninety-three hundred
9,400	nine thousand four hundred/ninety-four hundred
9,500	nine thousand five hundred/ninety-five hundred
9,600	nine thousand six hundred/ninety-six hundred
9,700	nine thousand seven hundred/ninety-seven hundred
9,800	nine thousand eight hundred/ninety-eight hundred
9,900	nine thousand nine hundred/ninety-nine hundred

CHAPTER 2 ▼ 大きな数字 ―3桁区切りに慣れる―

問題 1 ▶ 書き取り

解答は93ページ

次の数字の英語の発音を書きましょう。

1. 1,009

2. 3,303

3. 4,500

4. 5,050

5. 6,001

6. 12,000

7. 52,030

8. 63,000

9. 91,000

10. 33,561

11. 590,000

CHAPTER 2 ▼ 大きな数字 ―3桁区切りに慣れる―

12. 668,000

13. 333,300

14. 991,200

15. 123,456

次の音声を聞き、その数字を書きましょう。　　))) Track 069

1.

2.

3.

4.

5.

6.

7.

8.

9.

10.

11.

12.

13.

14.

15.

次の音声を聞き、空欄を埋めましょう。　　　))) Track 070

1. This theater has a maximum seating capacity of
[　　　　　].

2. A maximum of [　　　　　] guests can stay in
this hotel.

3. The seating capacity of this soccer stadium is
[　　　　　].

4. The population of my hometown is
[　　　　　].

5. About [　　　　　] people watched the
marathon race on the streets.

6. A:What does the [　　　　　] visitor to the
Ukiyoe Art Gallery get?

B:The [　　　　　] visitor can get a
woodblock print of Hiroshige.

7.

A：You are the [   ] graduate of this school.

B：How lucky I am!

8.

A：You are the [   ] guest at this movie theater.

B：Am I getting anything for that?

9.

A：How many people joined the anti-war demonstrations?

B：I heard on the radio that there were close to [   ] demonstrators.

10.

A：Many jazz lovers will get together at the free jazz concert held in Central Park this year.

B：You are right, about [   ] people joined the concert last year.

問題 1 ▶ 書き取り

1. one thousand (and) nine
2. three thousand three hundred (and) three
3. four thousand (and) five hundred/forty-five hundred
4. five thousand (and) fifty
5. six thousand (and) one
6. twelve thousand
7. fifty-two thousand (and) thirty
8. sixty-three thousand
9. ninety-one thousand
10. thirty-three thousand five hundred (and) sixty-one
11. five hundred ninety thousand
12. six hundred sixty-eight thousand
13. three hundred thirty-three thousand (and) three hundred
14. nine hundred ninety-one thousand (and) two hundred
15. one hundred twenty-three thousand four hundred (and) fifty-six

問題 2 ▶ 聞き取り

1.	8,900	6.	10,500	11.	100,002
2.	5,450	7.	61,000	12.	560,890
3.	6,894	8.	98,050	13.	960,000
4.	2,890	9.	77,200	14.	234,098
5.	1,902	10.	34,605	15	600,860

1. This theater has a maximum seating capacity of 5,000.
2. A maximum of 1,200 guests can stay in this hotel.
3. The seating capacity of this soccer stadium is 75,000.
4. The population of my hometown is 11,540.
5. About 850,000 people watched the marathon race on the streets.
6. A：What does the 1,000th visitor to the Ukiyoe Art Gallery get?

   B：The 1,000th visitor can get a woodblock print of Hiroshige.
7. A：You are the 22,222nd graduate of this school.

   B：How lucky I am!
8. A：You are the 99,999th guest at this movie theater.

   B：Am I getting anything for that?
9. A：How many people joined the anti-war demonstrations?

   B：I heard on the radio that there were close to 500,000
   demonstrators.
10. A：Many jazz lovers will get together at the free jazz concert held
    in Central Park this year.

    B：You are right, about 110,000 people joined the concert last year.

1. この劇場の最大着席収容者数は5千人です。
2. このホテルには最高で1,200人の宿泊客が泊まることができます。
3. このサッカースタジアムの収容人数は75,000人です。
4. 私の生まれた街の人口は11,540人です。
5. 約85万人が道路上でそのマラソンレースを見ました。
6. A：その浮世絵美術館の千人目の来館者は何をもらえますか？

B：千人目の来館者は広重の浮世絵の版画をもらえます。

7.　A：あなたはこの学校の22,222人目の卒業生です。

　　B：私はなんて幸運なのでしょう。

8.　A：あなたはこの映画館の99,999人目の入場者です。

　　B：何かもらえるのですか？

9.　A：その戦争反対のデモには何人の参加者がいましたか？

　　B：ラジオで聞いたのですが、50万人近い人がそのデモに参加した
　　　　そうです。

10.　A：セントラル・パークで開催される今年の無料のジャズコンサー
　　　　トにはたくさんのジャズ愛好家が集まるでしょうね。

　　B：あなたの言う通りです。昨年は約11万人がコンサートに参加し
　　　　ました。

02 ▶ million

2つめのコンマはmillionです。百万の1,000,000はone millionで、1千万の10,000,000はten million、1億の100,000,000はhundred millionと読みます。

音声を聞いて読み方を確認しましょう。　))) **Track** 071

1,000,000	one million
2,000,000	two million
3,000,000	three million
4,000,000	four million
5,000,000	five million
6,000,000	six million
7,000,000	seven million
8,000,000	eight million
9,000,000	nine million

))) **Track** 072

10,000,000	ten million
20,000,000	twenty million

30,000,000	thirty million
40,000,000	forty million
50,000,000	fifty million
60,000,000	sixty million
70,000,000	seventy million
80,000,000	eighty million
90,000,000	ninety million

))) Track 073

100,000,000	one hundred million
200,000,000	two hundred million
300,000,000	three hundred million
400,000,000	four hundred million
500,000,000	five hundred million
600,000,000	six hundred million
700,000,000	seven hundred million
800,000,000	eight hundred million
900,000,000	nine hundred million

反復練習 1 ▶ 桁サポート付

音声を聞き、声に出してくり返し練習しましょう。

1,000,000
million | thousand

10,000,000
million | thousand

100,000,000
million | thousand

2,000,000
million | thousand

30,000,000
million | thousand

400,000,000
million | thousand

CHAPTER 2 ▼ 大きな数字 ―3桁区切りに慣れる―

one million

ten million

one hundred million

two million

thirty million

four hundred million

音声を聞き、声に出してくり返し練習しましょう。

1,000,000

10,000,000

100,000,000

2,000,000

30,000,000

400,000,000

one million

ten million

one hundred million

two million

thirty million

four hundred million

反復練習3 ▶ もっと練習

音声を聞き、声に出してくり返し練習しましょう。　))) Track 076

1,000,000	one million
2,000,000	two million
3,000,000	three million
4,000,000	four million
5,000,000	five million
6,000,000	six million
7,000,000	seven million
8,000,000	eight million
9,000,000	nine million

))) Track 077

10,000,000	ten million
20,000,000	twenty million
30,000,000	thirty million
40,000,000	forty million

CHAPTER 2 ▼ 大きな数字 ──3桁区切りに慣れる──

50,000,000	fifty million
60,000,000	sixty million
70,000,000	seventy million
80,000,000	eighty million
90,000,000	ninety million

))) Track 078

100,000,000	one hundred million
200,000,000	two hundred million
300,000,000	three hundred million
400,000,000	four hundred million
500,000,000	five hundred million
600,000,000	six hundred million
700,000,000	seven hundred million
800,000,000	eight hundred million
900,000,000	nine hundred million

1,005,109	one million five thousand one hundred (and) nine
2,100,300	two million one hundred thousand (and) three hundred
3,300,123	three million three hundred thousand one hundred (and) twenty-three
4,555,666	four million five hundred fifty-five thousand six hundred (and) sixty-six
5,005,900	five million five thousand (and) nine hundred, five million (and) fifty nine hundred
6,070,001	six million seventy thousand (and) one
7,120,900	seven million one hundred twenty thousand (and) nine hundred
8,080,111	eight million eighty thousand one hundred (and) eleven
9,980,010	nine million nine hundred eighty thousand (and) ten
999,999,999	nine hundred ninety-nine million nine hundred ninety-nine thousand nine hundred (and) ninety-nine

次の数字の英語の発音を書きましょう。

1.　9,000,000

2.　8,111,000

3.　1,234,000

4.　4,500,000

5.　7,300,100

6.　20,100,500

7.　45,500,100

8. 90,300,001

9. 50,100,100

10. 60,001,999

11. 100,100,100

12. 220,000,222

13. 300,300,300

14. 405,500,000

15. 560,000,500

次の音声を聞き、その数字を書きましょう。))) Track 080

1.

2.

3.

4.

5.

6.

7.

8.

9.

10.

11.

CHAPTER 2 ▶ 大きな数字 —3桁区切りに慣れる—

12.

13.

14.

15.

次の音声を聞き、空欄を埋めましょう。))) Track 081

1.
A：How many cities with a population of
[　　　　　　　　] are there in this country?
B：There are [　　　　] cities with a population of
[　　　　] or more in this country.

2.
A：How many countries are there in the world that have a population of more than
[　　　　　　　　] people?
B：I don't know for sure, but I think there are about a dozen countries.

3.
A：How many countries in the world do you think have a population between
[　　　　　　] and
[　　　　　　]?
B：I just don't know.
A：Actually, I also don't know the exact figure, but I think there are many countries with a population that falls in that category.

A：How much did the population in the country
  increase over the past [   ] years?

4.　B：The country's population has increased by
  [   ] over the past [   ]
  years.

A：What are the populations of Japan and the
  U.S.A.?

5.　B：Japan has a population of about
  [   ], and the U.S.A. has a
  population of [   ].

問題1 ▶ 書き取り

1. nine million
2. eight million one hundred (and) eleven thousand
3. one million two hundred (and) thirty-four thousand
4. four million (and) five hundred thousand
5. seven million three hundred thousand (and) one hundred
6. twenty million one hundred thousand (and) five hundred
7. forty-five million five hundred thousand (and) one hundred
8. ninety million three hundred thousand (and) one
9. fifty million one hundred thousand (and) one hundred
10. sixty million one thousand nine hundred (and) ninety-nine
11. one hundred million one hundred thousand (and) one hundred
12. two hundred twenty million two hundred (and) twenty-two
13. three hundred million three hundred thousand (and) three hundred
14. four hundred five million (and) five hundred thousand
15. five hundred sixty million (and) five hundred

 問題2 ▶ 聞き取り

1.	1,600,100	6.	6,540,000	11.	770,770,770
2.	5,550,000	7.	2,000,001	12.	890,120,300
3.	9,112,800	8.	3,700,700	13.	999,100,009
4.	8,450,000	9.	4,440,130	14.	101,500,000
5.	7,234,500	10.	1,000,008	15.	600,000,006

(?) 問題 3 ▶ 空欄埋め

1. A: How many cities with a population of 1,000,000 are there in this country?

   B: There are twelve cities with a population of one million or more in this country.

2. A: How many countries are there in the world that have a population of more than 100 million people?

   B: I don't know for sure, but I think there are about a dozen countries.

3. A: How many countries in the world do you think have a population between 10 million and 90 million?

   B: I just don't know.

   A: Actually, I also don't know the exact figure, but I think there are many countries with a population that falls in that category.

4. A: How much did the population in the country increase over the past 50 years?

   B: The country's population has increased by 60 million over the past 50 years.

5. A: What are the populations of Japan and the U.S.A.?

   B: Japan has a population of about 126 million, and the U.S.A. has a population of 327 million.

....

1. A：この国で100万人以上の市はいくつありますか？

   B：人口100万人以上の市は全部で12あります。

2. A：世界に1億人以上の人口のいる国は、どのくらいありますか？

　　B：確実ではありませんが、12カ国くらいあるはずです。

 dozen=1ダース=12

3. A：世界の国の中で、人口が1千万人から9千万人いる国の数はどの
　　　くらいあると思いますか？

　　B：私にはわかりません。

　　A：実際には、私にもわからないのですが、その人口のレンジに入
　　　る国はたくさんあるはずです。

4. A：その国の人口はこの50年でどのくらい増加したのですか？

　　B：その国の人口はこの50年間で、6千万人増加しました。

5. A：日本と米国の人口はどのくらいですか？

　　B：日本の人口は1億2,600万人で、アメリカは3億2,700万人です。

03 ▸ billion

3つめのコンマはbillionです。1,000,000,000はone billionと読みます。
日本語では10億になります。
音声を聞き、読み方を確認しましょう。))) Track 082

1,000,000,000	one billion
2,000,000,000	two billion
3,000,000,000	three billion
4,000,000,000	four billion
5,000,000,000	five billion
6,000,000,000	six billion
7,000,000,000	seven billion
8,000,000,000	eight billion
9,000,000,000	nine billion

))) Track 083

| 10,000,000,000 | ten billion |
| 20,000,000,000 | twenty billion |

30,000,000,000	thirty billion
40,000,000,000	forty billion
50,000,000,000	fifty billion
60,000,000,000	sixty billion
70,000,000,000	seventy billion
80,000,000,000	eighty billion
90,000,000,000	ninety billion

100,000,000,000	one hundred billion
200,000,000,000	two hundred billion
300,000,000,000	three hundred billion
400,000,000,000	four hundred billion
500,000,000,000	five hundred billion
600,000,000,000	six hundred billion
700,000,000,000	seven hundred billion
800,000,000,000	eight hundred billion
900,000,000,000	nine hundred billion

音声を聞き、声に出してくり返し練習しましょう。

1,000,000,000
billion　million　thousand

10,000,000,000
billion　million　thousand

100,000,000,000
billion　million　thousand

2,000,000,000
billion　million　thousand

30,000,000,000
billion　million　thousand

400,000,000,000
billion　million　thousand

CHAPTER 2 ▼ 大きな数字 ──3桁区切りに慣れる──

one billion

ten billion

one hundred billion

two billion

thirty billion

four hundred billion

音声を聞き、声に出してくり返し練習しましょう。

1,000,000,000

10,000,000,000

100,000,000,000

2,000,000,000

30,000,000,000

400,000,000,000

one billion

ten billion

one hundred billion

two billion

thirty billion

four hundred billion

反復練習 3 ▶ もっと練習

音声を聞き、声に出してくり返し練習しましょう。　))) **Track** 087

1,000,000,000	one billion
2,000,000,000	two billion
3,000,000,000	three billion
4,000,000,000	four billion
5,000,000,000	five billion
6,000,000,000	six billion
7,000,000,000	seven billion
8,000,000,000	eight billion
9,000,000,000	nine billion

))) **Track** 088

10,000,000,000	ten billion
20,000,000,000	twenty billion
30,000,000,000	thirty billion
40,000,000,000	forty billion

CHAPTER 2 ▼ 大きな数字 ―3桁区切りに慣れる―

50,000,000,000	fifty billion
60,000,000,000	sixty billion
70,000,000,000	seventy billion
80,000,000,000	eighty billion
90,000,000,000	ninety billion

))) Track 089

100,000,000,000	one hundred billion
200,000,000,000	two hundred billion
300,000,000,000	three hundred billion
400,000,000,000	four hundred billion
500,000,000,000	five hundred billion
600,000,000,000	six hundred billion
700,000,000,000	seven hundred billion
800,000,000,000	eight hundred billion
900,000,000,000	nine hundred billion

問題 1 ▶ 書き取り

解答は129ページ

次の数字の英語の発音を書きましょう。

....

1. 8,900,100,000

....

2. 5,005,005,009

....

CHAPTER 2 ▼ 大きな数字 ―3桁区切りに慣れる―

3. 3,000,000,001

....

4. 8,000,000,121

....

5. 5,000,004,000

....

6.   2,000,200,200

7.   9,000,555,005

8.   20,900,100,000

9.   90,000,000,800

10.   55,009,095,000

11. 717,000,700,300

12. 120,900,700,000

13. 800,100,000,700

14. 550,003,045,000

15. 613,000,000,007

次の音声を聞き、その数字を書きましょう。　))) Track 090

....

1.

....

2.

....

3.

....

4.

....

5.

....

6.

....

7.

....

8.

9.

10.

11.

CHAPTER 2 ▼ 大きな数字 ―3桁区切りに慣れる―

12.

13.

14.

15.

次の音声を聞き、空欄を埋めましょう。　　　))) Track 091

1.

A：How many people are expected to watch the soccer game in the world?

B：[　　　　　　　　　　] people worldwide are expected to watch the game on TV.

2.

A：How old is the earth?

B：The birth of the earth dates back to [　　　　　　　　　　] years ago, plus or minus [　　　　　　　] years.

3.

A：The figures between [　　　　　　　　　] and [　　　　　　　　　] are so large we don't often encounter them in daily life.

B：Yes, I agree with you.

A : Do you know how many stars there are in the Galaxy?

B : I don't have the faintest idea. Do you?

4.

A : The Galaxy is believed to consist of between

[   ] and

[   ] stars.

A : How many conversations take place between messenger users and businesses every month?

5.

B : In any given month, there are over

[   ] conversations.

問題 1 ▶ 書き取り

1. eight billion nine hundred million one hundred thousand
2. five billion five million five thousand (and) nine
3. three billion (and) one
4. eight billion one hundred (and) twenty-one
5. five billion four thousand
6. two billion two hundred thousand two hundred
7. nine billion five hundred fifty-five thousand (and) five
8. twenty billion nine hundred million one hundred thousand
9. ninety billion eight hundred
10. fifty-five billion nine million ninety-five thousand
11. seven hundred seventeen billion seven hundred thousand three hundred
12. one hundred twenty billion, nine hundred million, seven hundred thousand
13. eight hundred billion one hundred million seven hundred
14. five hundred fifty billion three million forty-five thousand
15. six hundred thirteen billion (and) seven

 問題 2 ▶ 聞き取り

1. 6,000,700,600
2. 7,800,900,000
3. 9,000,900,800
4. 4,004,005,006
5. 3,000,000,333
6. 88,000,000,887
7. 35,000,400,000
8. 41,444,555,000
9. 72,000,700,800
10. 19,000,000,009
11. 870,000,700,787
12. 235,100,100,000
13. 441,777,666,000
14. 272,000,200,200
15. 900,000,000,001

❓ 問題 3 ▶ 空欄埋め

1. A：How many people are expected to watch the soccer game in
   the world?
   B：Two billion people worldwide are expected to watch the game
   on TV.

2. A：How old is the earth?
   B：The birth of the earth dates back to 4.54 billion years ago, plus
   or minus 50 million years.

3. A：The figures between ten billion and 90 billion are so large we
   don't often encounter them in daily life.
   B：Yes, I agree with you.

4. A：Do you know how many stars there are in the Galaxy?
   B：I don't have the faintest idea. Do you?
   A：The Galaxy is believed to consist of between 200 billion and
   400 billion stars.

5. A：How many conversations take place between messenger users
   and businesses every month?
   B：In any given month, there are over 2 billion conversations.

1. A：世界中でどのくらいの人がそのサッカーの試合を見ると予想さ
   れていますか？
   B：世界中で20億人の人が、その試合をテレビで見ると予想されて
   います。

2. A：地球は何歳くらいですか？
   B：地球の誕生は、45.4億年プラスマイナス5千万年前と言われてい

ます。

3. 　Ａ：百億から9百憶までの数字は、大きすぎるので日常生活で頻繁に
　　　　出会うものではありません。

　　Ｂ：あなたに同意します。

4. 　Ａ：銀河系にどのくらいの数の星があるかご存知ですか？

　　Ｂ：全く想像がつきません。知っていますか。

　　Ａ：銀河系は2千億から4千億の星で成り立っていると考えられてい
　　　　ます。

5. 　Ａ：メッセンジャーアプリでのユーザーと商用アカウントとの間で
　　　　は、毎月どの位のやりとりがありますか？

　　Ｂ：一月当たり20億以上の会話があります。

04 ▶ trillion

4つめのコンマは trillion です。1,000,000,000,000 は one trillion と読みます。日本語では1兆になります。

音声を聞き、読み方を確認しましょう。

))) **Track** 092

1,000,000,000,000	one trillion
2,000,000,000,000	two trillion
3,000,000,000,000	three trillion
4,000,000,000,000	four trillion
5,000,000,000,000	five trillion
6,000,000,000,000	six trillion
7,000,000,000,000	seven trillion
8,000,000,000,000	eight trillion
9,000,000,000,000	nine trillion

10,000,000,000,000 ten trillion

20,000,000,000,000 twenty trillion

30,000,000,000,000 thirty trillion

40,000,000,000,000 forty trillion

50,000,000,000,000 fifty trillion

60,000,000,000,000 sixty trillion

70,000,000,000,000 seventy trillion

80,000,000,000,000 eighty trillion

90,000,000,000,000 ninety trillion

音声を聞き、声に出してくり返し練習しましょう。

1,000,000,000,000
trillion　billion　million　thousand

10,000,000,000,000
trillion　billion　million　thousand

2,000,000,000,000
trillion　billion　million　thousand

3,000,000,000,000
trillion　billion　million　thousand

40,000,000,000,000
trillion　billion　million　thousand

50,000,000,000,000
trillion　billion　million　thousand

CHAPTER 2 ▼ 大きな数字 —3桁区切りに慣れる—

one trillion

ten trillion

two trillion

three trillion

forty trillion

fifty trillion

音声を聞き、声に出してくり返し練習しましょう。

1,000,000,000,000

10,000,000,000,000

2,000,000,000,000

3,000,000,000,000

40,000,000,000,000

50,000,000,000,000

one trillion

ten trillion

two trillion

three trillion

forty trillion

fifty trillion

反復練習3 ▶ もっと練習

音声を聞き、声に出してくり返し練習しましょう。))) Track 096

1,000,000,000,000	one trillion
2,000,000,000,000	two trillion
3,000,000,000,000	three trillion
4,000,000,000,000	four trillion
5,000,000,000,000	five trillion
6,000,000,000,000	six trillion
7,000,000,000,000	seven trillion
8,000,000,000,000	eight trillion
9,000,000,000,000	nine trillion

))) Track 097

10,000,000,000,000	ten trillion
20,000,000,000,000	twenty trillion
30,000,000,000,000	thirty trillion

40,000,000,000,000 forty trillion

50,000,000,000,000 fifty trillion

60,000,000,000,000 sixty trillion

70,000,000,000,000 seventy trillion

80,000,000,000,000 eighty trillion

90,000,000,000,000 ninety trillion

次の数字の英語の発音を書きましょう。

1.　　7,000,000,100,900

2.　　1,120,800,400,000

3.　　2,800,900,000,100

4.　　5,550,002,075,000

5.　　6,626,000,000,006

6.   10,800,000,000,121

7.   50,000,001,000,000

8.   10,234,000,000,100

9.   22,000,200,200,000

10.   90,000,555,005,000

次の音声を聞き、その数字を書きましょう。　　))) Track 098

1.

2.

3.

4.

5.

6.

7.

8.

....

9.

....

10.

....

? 問題 3 ▸ 空欄埋め　　　　　　　　　　　解答は145ページ

次の音声を聞き、空欄を埋めましょう。　　　　))) Track 099

....

A：Do you know how many human cells are used to make one human body?

B：You're asking the wrong person.

A：Actually, the number of human cells was once believed to be about [　　　　　　　　　　], but now the number has been reduced to some [　　　　　　　　　　].

B：That number is still astronomical.

....

▶ 解答・日本語訳

 問題 1 ▶ 書き取り

1. seven trillion one hundred thousand nine hundred
2. one trillion one hundred twenty billion eight hundred million four hundred thousand
3. two trillion eight hundred billion nine hundred million one hundred
4. five trillion five hundred fifty billion two million seventy-five thousand
5. six trillion six hundred twenty-six billion (and) six
6. ten trillion eight hundred billion one hundred (and) twenty-one
7. fifty trillion one million
8. ten trillion two hundred thirty-four billion one hundred
9. twenty-two trillion two hundred million two hundred thousand
10. ninety trillion five hundred fifty-five million five thousand

 問題 2 ▶ 聞き取り

1. 8,070,000,900,111
2. 2,035,600,300,000
3. 4,444,999,333,000
4. 3,272,000,300,400
5. 9,800,000,000,007
6. 80,000,000,000,111
7. 50,100,000,005,000
8. 10,000,234,000,000
9. 20,000,200,100,200
10. 90,000,000,444,002

問題 3 ▶ 空欄埋め

A：Do you know how many human cells are used to make one human body?

B：You're asking the wrong person.

A：Actually, the number of human cells was once believed to be about 60 trillion, but now the number has been reduced to some 37 trillion.

B：That number is still astronomical.

A：人間の体を作るのにどのくらいの細胞が使われているか、知っていますか？

B：聞く相手を間違っていますよ。

A：人体細胞の数は、かつては60兆個と言われていましたが、その数が 37兆個に減りました。

B：それでもまだ天文学的数字ですね。

たくさんある「たくさんの」

CHPTER 2では、thousand, million, billion, trillion という大きな数字を覚えました。これらは、ただ大きな数字を表す単位というだけでなく、「たくさんの」や「とても大きな数字」を表現したいときにも使うことができます。

■hundreds of thousands of　非常にたくさんの

Hundreds of thousands of people were at the fair.

そのお祭りにはとてもたくさんの人がいました。

■thousands of　とても多くの、何千回も、2,000以上

A：Have you tried this method?

B：Yes, I've done that thousands of times.

A：このやり方はトライしましたか？

B：それは、何度も何度もやりました。

■billions of　とても大きな数字、何十億の

Our immune systems are killing billions of germs right now.

我々の免疫システムは、たった今もものすごい数の細菌を殺しているのです。

■billions and billions of　とても大きな数字

They saw billions and billions of stars in the sky on the small island.

彼らはその小さな島で、空にものすごい数の星を見た。

■trillions of　とても大きな数字

We could see trillions of stars in the sky.

私たちはものすごい数の星を見ることができた。

■trillions and trillions of　とても大きな数字、数え切れないほど大きな数字

Human bodies are made of trillions and trillions of cells.

人間の体は数え切れないほど多くの細胞でできている。

CHAPTER

3

....

数字を使って伝える

01

▶ お金

アメリカとイギリスのお金の名称

アメリカのお金の呼び方は基本的にドル（$）です。ドルを使っている国は他にもあり、オーストラリアドル、ニュージーランドドル、シンガポールドル、香港ドルなどが存在します。一方、イギリスはポンド（£）です。

札の呼び方

紙幣はアメリカでは bill、イギリスでは note と呼びます。　　))) Track 100

アメリカ	イギリス
one-dollar bill	
two-dollar bill	
five-dollar bill	five-pound note
ten-dollar bill	ten-pound note
twenty-dollar bill	twenty-pound note
fifty-dollar bill	fifty-pound note
hundred-dollar bill	

コインの呼び方

硬貨はアメリカでもイギリスでも coin です。

アメリカ	イギリス
cent, penny	penny
	two pence
five-cent, nickel	five pence
ten-cent, dime	ten pence
	twenty pence
quarter dollar, quarter	
half-dollar, half	fifty pence
dollar coin	one pound

アメリカでは、1セントのことをpenny（ペニー）、5セントのことをnickel（ニッケル）、10セントは、アメリカで1番小さいサイズのコインでdime（ダイム）と呼びます。25セントは、1ドルの4分の1を意味するquarter（クォーター）、50セントは、half dollar またはそのまま fifty cents と呼びます。

硬貨そのものについて言う場合は、penny が複数形になると pennies になります。アメリカにある25セントに相当するコインはイギリスにはなく、一方、アメリカにない2ペンスがイギリスにはあります。

日本の1万円に相当する呼び方は英米にはなく、1万ドルは1,000ドルが10個あることを意味する ten thousand、10万ドルは、1,000ドルが100個あることを意味する one hundred thousand と呼びます。この呼び方は、口から自然にでるようになるまで、普段から練習しておくことが大切です。英語で大きい数を言ったり聞いたりすることに慣れておきましょう。特にビジネスにおいては、金額を間違えずに正しく言えることが必須です。

ちなみに、英語には1,000ドル/ポンドを意味する grand という言葉があります。これは単数形も複数形も同じです。これを使うと、1万ドルは ten grand となります。日常会話ではよく使われる表現です。

お金の数え方 　　　　　　　　　　　　　　　　　))) Track 102

$/£1	one dollar
	one pound
$/£10	ten dollars
	ten pounds
$/£100	one hundred dollars
	one hundred pounds
$/£1,000	one thousand dollars, one grand
	one thousand pounds, one grand

$/£10,000	ten thousand dollars, ten grand
	ten thousand pounds, ten grand
$/£100,000	hundred thousand dollars
	hundred thousand pounds
$/£1,000,000	one million dollars
	one million pounds
$/£10,000,000	ten million dollars
	ten million pounds
$/£100,000,000	hundred million dollars
	hundred million pounds
$/£1000,000,000	one billion dollars
	one billion pounds

☐ **I will sell this car at six thousand pounds.**
この車は6,000ポンドで売ります。

☐ **We spend four hundred and fifty pounds a month on food.**
食事に月に£450使います。

☐ **We are saving two hundred dollars each month for education allowances for my two children.**
私たちは子どもたちの教育資金として一人当たり毎月200ドル貯金しています。

☐ **Have you got change for a $50 bill?**
50ドル札でお釣りはありますか?

📖 change お釣り

That large car company was five billion dollars in the red two years ago.

あの大手の自動車会社は、2年前50億ドルの赤字でした。

in the red 赤字／in the black 黒字

I sold our house for 350 grand.

私は家を35万ドルで売りました。

We spent $ 50,000 on our daughter's university tuition every year.

私たちは娘の大学の学費に毎年5万ドルついやした。

He made two million dollars in profit in the stock market.

彼は株で2百万ドルの利益を得た。

問題 1 ▶ 書き取り   解答は157ページ

次の数字の英語の発音を書きましょう。

....

1. $ 80

....

2.   £ 120

....

154

CHAPTER 3 ▼ 数字を使って伝える

3. $ 9,000

....

4. $ 20,000

....

5.   £ 72,000

....

次の音声を聞き、その数字を書きましょう。　　　))) Track 104

1.

2.

3.

4.

5.

次の音声を聞き、空欄を埋めましょう。　　　)))**Track** 105

1. The price of this watch is [　　　　　].

2. The final price with the discount comes to
   [　　　　].

3. We were [　　　　　　　　　] in
   the red last year.

4. Our **initial** monthly **salary** is [　　　　　].

📖 initial salary 初任給

5. A：How much does it come to in all?
   B：It comes to [　　　　] in all, or [　　　　] per
   person.

問題1 ▶ 書き取り

1. eighty dollars
2. a/one hundred twenty pounds
3. nine grand/thousand dollars
4. twenty grand/thousand dollars
5. seventy-two grand/thousand pounds

問題2 ▶ 聞き取り

1. $ 400
2. £ 33
3. $ 5,000
4. $ 6,000,000
5. £ 89,000

1. The price of this watch is $49.50.

2. The final price with the discount comes to $294.

3. We were 10 million dollars in the red last year.

4. Our initial monthly salary is $2,500.

5. A: How much does it come to in all?

   B: It comes to £94 in all, or £47 per person.

---

1. この時計の値段は49ドル50セントです。

2. 割引後の最終価格は294ドルになります。

3. 私たちは、昨年1千万ドルの赤字でした。

4. わが社の月の初任給は2,500ドルです。

5. A：全部でいくらになりますか？

   B：全部で94ポンド、または一人あたり47ポンドです。

日本と欧米のお金に関する違い

日米の家庭で夫か妻のどちらが家計を管理しているか、その割合をネットで調べてみました。色々な数字があって、はっきりしたことは分かりませんでしたが、わかった範囲での結論としては、妻が家計を管理しているのは、アメリカでは24%、日本では72%ということでした。この数字からわかることは、アメリカでは夫が、日本では妻が、家計を管理しているということです。

アメリカの子どもたちは男女を問わず、色々なアルバイトをしてお金を稼ぎます。代表的なアルバイトとしては、近所や自分の家の芝刈り、ベビーシッティング、家事の手伝いやペットの世話、新聞配達、レモネードの屋台店での販売などです。お金は自動的に両親からお小遣いとしてもらうものではなく、自分が働いた報酬として稼ぎ出すものだという意識を強く持つようになります。従って、とても小さい金額についても、こだわります。結婚すると、80%くらいのアメリカ人男性は、家計を一手に握ります。

もうひとつ日本と違うのが、チップの習慣です。日本にはチップの習慣がないので、なぜチップが必要なのかを説明します。アメリカのウェイターやウェイトレスの給料は低く、それだけではなかなか豊かな暮らしはできません。例えば、州によって違いますが、1時間当たりの最低賃金は11ドルから12ドルくらいです。5時間働いても、60ドルくらいです。一方、高級レストランのウェイター・ウェイトレスは、1日に100ドルから200ドルくらいのチップをもらえます。もちろん個人差がありますが、いいサービスをする人は特にたくさんもらいます。このチップが、彼らの主な収入源になります。従って、チップをもらえないと収入が3分の2も減ってしまうことになります。

New York Times が掲載している Tipping Guide（チップの相場表）をご紹介します。アメリカに行った際に、参考にしてください。

職業	チップの%または金額
ウェイター・ウェイトレス	15％-20％
ソムリエ	ボトル代の15%-20%
ベルボーイ	バッグ1個2ドル（高級ホテル） バッグ1個1ドル（普通のホテル）
ホテルの客室清掃	1日2ドル
ドアマン	1-2ドル（タクシーを呼ぶ費用）
タクシー運転手	15％-20％

02 ▶ 電話番号

電話番号は、日常生活はもちろん、ビジネスシーンでも非常に重要です。数字をひとつ聞き間違えるだけで、トラブルにつながってしまうこともあります。この本でしっかり練習して、間違いなく聞き取れる・伝えられるようになりましょう。

電話番号の読み方には一定のルールがあります。たとえば、322-1555を three two two, one five five five と言ってももちろん通じます。しかし、同じ数字が2つ並ぶ場合にはその前に double を、3つ並ぶ場合には triple を付けて読むことがよくあります。欧米人が、このような読み方をするのを頭の中に入れて置くことが大切です。このルールを使うと、次のように読みます。

322-1555 　three double two, one triple five

また、アメリカでは5セント硬貨のことを nickel と呼びますが、これを使って、1555を one triple nickel と読む人もいます。

0が並ぶ場合にも、読み方のルールがあります。たとえば201-3000は、two zero one, three zero zero zero と読んでも通じます。しかし、two zero one, three thousand と読むのが一般的です。200-0200は、two hundred, zero two hundred と読みます。

ちなみに、0を oh と読む人がいますが、4（four）と聞き間違えることが、欧米人の間でもあるので、必ず zero と読むようにしてください。たとえば、次の電話番号を読んでみてください。

204-4040

two oh four, four oh four oh では間違いやすいので、必ず、two zero four, four zero four zero と読む癖をつけてください。ちなみに、日本式の電話番

号の読み方で「-」を「の」と読みますが、英語では「-」を読みません。また、電話番号の数字を読むときには、2桁ずつ読むのが一般的です。3147-8569 は three one four seven, eight five six nine ではなく、thirty-one forty-seven, eighty-five sixty-nine を分けて読むことが多いです。13 は thirteen と読むと30の thirty と間違われやすいので、13 thirteen not three zero, but one three のように、あとで確認するのが大切です。14と40、15と50等も間違いやすいので、40と言った後では、four zero、50と言った後では、five zero のように言い直すようにしてください。13と30等の発音はかなり近く、13をサーティーン、30をサーティのようにはっきりとはわかりにくいのが普通です。

それでは、電話番号を声に出して読んでみましょう。
国際電話の場合、頭に日本の国番号81をつけ、電話番号の最初の0をとります。

))) **Track** 106

CHAPTER 3 ▼ 数字を使って伝える

1.	**81-45-3302-1440**	eighty-one, forty-five, double three zero two, one four four zero
2.	**03-3011-0404**	zero three, three zero one one, zero four zero four
3.	**045-1330-4014**	zero four five, one three three zero, four zero one four
4.	**232-1000-2010**	two three two, one thousand, two zero one zero
5.	**090-1204-3010**	zero nine zero, one two zero four, three zero one zero

次の電話番号の英語の読み方を書きましょう。

1.　　03-3312-9000

2.　　045-772-4040

3.　　81-3-2400-0555

4.　　212-8983-0300

5.　　689-1122-2001

次の音声を聞き、電話番号を書きましょう。　　　))) Track 107

1.

2.

3.

4.

5.

次の音声を聞き、空欄を埋めましょう。　　　))) Track 108

1.
A：Good morning. How can I help you?

B：Good morning, this is Watson from ABC company. May I speak to Ms. Watanabe?

A：I'm sorry, Ms. Watanabe is in a meeting until 12.

B：Well, could you ask her to call me back when she returns? My number is
[　　　　　　　　　　　　].

2.
A：I'll call you when the item arrives. Let me repeat your phone number.

It's [　　　　　　　　　]?

B：No, not three zero, it's one three.
[　　　　　　　　　　　　].

▶ 解答・日本語訳

🖉 問題 1 ▶ 書き取り

1. zero three double three one two nine thousand
2. zero four five double seven two four zero four zero
3. eighty-one three twenty-four hundred zero triple five
4. two one two eighty-nine eighty-three zero three hundred
5. six eight nine double one double two two zero zero one

🎧 問題 2 ▶ 聞き取り

1. 090-3344-9423
2. 080-7800-4567
3. 256-9080-1213
4. 06-1200-0500
5. 041-789-5577

❓ 問題 3 ▶ 空欄埋め

1. A: Good morning. How can I help you?

   B: Good morning, this is Watson from ABC company. May I speak to Ms. Watanabe?

   A: I'm sorry, Ms. Watanabe is in a meeting until 12.

   B: Well, could you ask her to call me back when she returns? My number is 072-584-2200.

2. A: I'll call you when the item arrives. Let me repeat your phone number. It's 06-3050-9478?

B：No, not three zero, it's one three. 06-1350-9478.

1. A：おはようございます。ご用件をお伺いいたします。
   B：おはようございます。ABCカンパニーのワトソンです。渡辺さんをお願いします。
   A：申し訳ございません。渡辺は12時まで会議に出席しております。
   B：では、戻られたら折り返しお電話いただけますでしょうか。私の番号は072-584-2200です。
2. A：商品が入荷したらご連絡いたします。電話番号を確認させてください。06-3050-9478でしょうか？
   B：いえ、30ではなく13です。06-1350-9478です。

▶ 西暦

紀元前はBC、西暦（紀元後）はADと書きます。BCはBefore Christ、つまりキリスト以前を表し、ADはAnno Dominiで、ラテン語でin the year of Our Lord我らの主（すなわちキリスト）の時代に、を意味します。実際には、キリストは紀元前4年に生まれたそうです。

最近は、キリスト教に関係のないBCE（Before the Common Era）、CE（Common Era）が使われるようになってきました。特に学問的な分野でその傾向が強いです。

BCは数字の後に、ADは前に書きます。紀元後を表すときは何も書かない場合もあります。

))) **Track** 109

200 BC	紀元前200年
75 BC	紀元前75年
350 BC,BCE three fifty BC or BCE	紀元前350年
(AD) 567	西暦567年
(AD) nineteen sixty-four	西暦1964年
AD fifteen, (the year) fifteen AD	西暦15年

また、アメリカとイギリス・オーストラリアとは読み方が次のように違っていることもありますので、覚えてください。 Track 110

1567年	fifteen sixty-seven	（英米）
1812年	eighteen twelve	（英米）
1962年	nineteen sixty-two	（英米）

0が入る場合　　　　　　　　　　　　　　　　　　　 Track 111

1407年	fourteen oh seven	（英米）
	fourteen hundred and seven	（英）
1901年	nineteen oh one	（英米）
	nineteen hundred and one	（英）
1900年	nineteen hundred	（英米）
2000年	(the year) two thousand	（英米）

2000は年数以外でも使われることが多いので、年数を意味していることを明らかにするために前にthe yearをつけます。

2000年以降は次のように言います。

))) **Track** 112

2003年	twenty oh three	（英米）
	two thousand and three	（英）

2010年	twenty ten	（英米）
	two thousand and ten	（英）

2019年	twenty nineteen	（英米）
	two thousand and nineteen	（英）

2020年	twenty twenty	（英米）
	two thousand and twenty	（英）

日本では最近2020年オリンピックのことを東京ニーゼロニーゼロ・オリンピックと呼んでいますが、英語では the twenty twenty Tokyo Olympics と言います。twenty twenty は、正常な視力のことも意味します。これは1/3インチ（約8ミリ）の大きさの字を20フィート（約6メートル）離れた場所から読める視力です。従って、2020は正常な視力の都市も意味することになります。

2100年	twenty-one hundred	（英米）

a millennium	千年間

two millennia (millenniums)	2千年間

 millennium の複数形は millennia、millenniums のどちらも使用可能です。

CHAPTER 3 ▼ 数字を使って伝える

～年代

in the 1980s (nineteen eighties)	1980年代に
in the early 1950s	1950年代初期に
in the mid-1970s	1970年代中頃に
in the late 1980s	1980年代後期に
in the year 2019	2019年に
during the 1990s	1990年代を通じて
throughout the 2000s	2000年代を通じてずっと
throughout the 2010s	2010年代を通じてずっと

twenty tens もしくは twenty teens とも発音します。

～世紀

Track 114

one/a century	1世紀
a half century/half a century	半世紀
a quarter century, **a quarter of a century**	四半世紀

the fifth century	5世紀
the first half of the 19th century	19世紀前半
the 20th century	20世紀
the last half of the 20th century	20世紀後半
the 21st century	21世紀

☐ **I was born in 1988.**

私は1988年生まれです。

☐ **I joined this company in 2011.**

私は2011年に入社しました。

☐ **This new bookstore opened in 2018.**

この新しい書店は2018年に開店しました。

☐ **I lived in Singapore from 1995 to 2004.**

1995年から2004年までシンガポールに住んでいました。

☐ **The church, built in the tenth century, has wonderful stained-glass windows.**

10世紀に建てられたその教会は、素晴らしいステンドグラスの窓がついている。

次の英語を和訳してください。また、音声を聞いて正しく発音してみましょう。　　　　　　　　　　　　　　　　　　　))) Track 116

1.　the early 8th century

2.　the mid-19th century

3.　BC 323

4.　in the late 1920s

5.　throughout the 2010s

次の日本語を英訳してください。

1. 9世紀

2. 前世紀

3. 西暦1868年に

4. 1970年代に

5. 2025年に

次の音声を聞き、空欄を埋めましょう。　　))) Track 117

1. The battle between the two countries lasted from [　　　　　] to [　　　　　].

2. My grandfather was born in [　　　　　].

3. This mansion was built in the late [　　　　　].

4. The old bridge was largely rebuilt in the [　　　　　] century.

5. A: When was the famous author born?

   B: He was born in Ireland in [　　　　　].

▶ 解答・日本語訳

 問題1 ▶ 書き取り（和訳）

1. 8世紀初め
2. 19世紀半ば
3. 紀元前323年
4. 1920年代後期に
5. 2010年代を通じてずっと

 問題2 ▶ 書き取り（英訳）

1. the ninth century
2. the last century
3. in (AD) 1868
4. in the 1970s
5. in twenty twenty-five/in 2025

1. The battle between the two countries lasted from 1337 to 1453.
2. My grandfather was born in 1913.
3. This mansion was built in the late 1940s.
4. The old bridge was largely rebuilt in the 18th century.
5. A: When was the famous author born?
   B: He was born in Ireland in 1832.

. . . .

1. その2カ国の戦いは1337年から1453年まで続いた。
2. 私の祖父は1913年に生まれた。
3. この大邸宅は1940年代後半に建設された。
4. その古い橋は18世紀に大幅に再建された。
5. A：その有名な作家はいつ生まれたのですか？
   B：彼は1832年にアイルランドで生まれました。

アメリカと、イギリス・オーストラリアでは日にちの表現が逆です。
例えば、5月4日は、アメリカでは5/4またはMay 4 (fourth)、と書きます が、イギリス・オーストラリアでは4/5または4th of Mayと書き、日にちと月が逆になっています。従って、日付を確認する際には十分注意しなければなりません。
アメリカとだけ連絡をしたり、イギリス系の国とだけ連絡をしたりするのであれば問題は起きませんが、それらが一緒になると混乱が生じます。

4月5日のアメリカ式とイギリス式の表示は次の通りです。

アメリカ式	イギリス式
4/5, April 5 (April fifth)	5/4, the 5th of April (the fifth of April)

混乱を避けるためには、4/5や5/4のような書き方ではなく、April fifthまたはthe fifth of Aprilのようにスペルアウトする必要があります。このようにすれば、4月5日なのか、5月4日なのか勘違いすることがないからです。納期交渉では特に大切で、絶対に数字だけで使わないようにしてください。

さらに例をあげます

	アメリカ式	イギリス式
3月10日	March 10th	the 10th of March
5月31日	May 31st	the 31st of May
11月20日付の あなたの手紙	your letter dated November 20th	your letter dated the 20th of November

〜年〜月〜日

January 1st, 2020/ 1st of January, 2020	2020年1月1日
on February 10th, 2022/ on the 10th of February 2022	2022年2月10日
on Saturday, March 16, 2019	2019年3月16日の土曜
the newspaper for April 2nd, 2023	2023年4月2日の新聞

))) Track 119

I was born on August 20th in the year 2000.

私は2000年の8月20日に生まれました。

This figure is as of September 7th, 2019.

この数字は2019年9月7日現在の数字です。

This contract will expire on December 31, 2022.

この契約書は2022年12月31日で終了します。

このように December 31 と書いても、December thirty-first のように読みます。January 1 であれば、January first と読みます。January 3 であれば、January third となります。

The next meeting will be held on the 14th of October.

次の会議は10月14日に実施されます。

My visa expires on the 22nd of January, 2021.

私のビザは2021年1月22日に失効します。

次の日付の英語の読み方を書きましょう。（アメリカ式で）

1. 　2月13日

2. 　1月1日

3. 　8月8日

4. 　10月11日

5. 　12月24日

次の音声を聞き、空欄を埋めましょう。　　　　))) **Track** 120

---

1. A：When is your birthday?

   B：My birthday is [　　　　　　　　　　　].

---

2. A：When is your wedding day?

   B：We've chosen

   [　　　　　　　　　　　　　　], as

   our wedding day.

---

3. A：On what date are your family leaving for
   London?

   B：Our family will leave a week from today, or

   [　　　　　　　　　　　　　　].

---

4. A：What is the date today?

   B：It's [　　　　　　　].

---

5. A：On what date in what year did you get married?

   B：I got married [　　　　　　　　　　].

▶ 解答・日本語訳

✏️ 問題1 ▶ 書き取り

1. February thirteenth
2. January first
3. August eighth
4. October eleventh
5. December twenty-fourth

❓ 問題2 ▶ 空欄埋め

1. A：When is your birthday?
   B：My birthday is the 10th of December.
2. A：When is your wedding day?
   B：We've chosen October 20th, 2020, as our wedding day.
3. A：On what date are your family leaving for London?
   B：Our family will leave a week from today, or September 21st, 2019.
4. A：What is the date today?
   B：It's the 31st of August.
5. A：On what date in what year did you get married?
   B：I got married May 30th, 1970.

. . . .

1. A：あなたの誕生日はいつですか？
   B：私の誕生日は12月10日です。
2. A：あなたの結婚式の日はいつですか？
   B：結婚式の日は、2020年の10月20日に決めました。

3. Ａ：あなたたち家族は何日にロンドンへ出発するのですか？
   Ｂ：私たち家族は今日から1週間後の2019年9月21日に出発します。
4. Ａ：今日は何日ですか？
   Ｂ：8月31日です。
5. Ａ：何年の何月に結婚しましたか？
   Ｂ：1970年の5月30日に結婚しました。

数字を使ったイディオム

数字を使ったイディオムを紹介します。日本語と同様の意味でも、数字が異なるものがいろいろありますね。

■twenty-four seven, 24-7, 24/7　年中無休の
1日24時間、週7日で、年中無休となるので、こう言います。

■six of one, half (a) dozen of the other　ふたつの間に違いは感じない
1が6個でも、12の半分でもどちらも同じ事という意味です。

■ninety-nine times out of a hundred　ほとんどいつも、十中八九、
本来の意味は100回のうち99回は、あることが起こることを意味しています。

■A picture is worth a thousand words.　一枚の絵を見ることは一千語に値する
日本語の「百聞は一見にしかず」と同様の意味で使われます。

■in seventh heaven　無上の幸福に浸る
ユダヤ教で神と天使のいる場所と考えられている第七天（7番目の天国）が由来となっています。

■bottom of the ninth　最後の最後の
野球の9回裏に例えた表現です。

■third time lucky　3度目の正直
日本語でも「3度目の正直」といいますよね。2回まではだめでも3回目はうまくいくという意味です。

■seven-year itch　7年目の浮気
日本には「3年目の浮気」という歌がありますが、英語では7年目です。結婚して7年くらいすると、浮気の虫が動き始めるのではないかという考えにちなんだ言い回しです。1955年にマリリン・モンローが主演した映画のタイトルにもなっています。

■eleventh-hour　土壇場の、ぎりぎりの、
11時を意味するわけではなく、締め切りぎりぎりの時間を表します。これ以外の数字は使いません。聖書が由来になっているようです。

years old 何歳

ten years old, ten years of age 10歳

 ten years of age の方が、より正式な言い方です。

a ten-year-old ～ 10歳/10年の～

a ten-year-old house 築10年の家

push そろそろ～歳になる

I'm pushing 30.

そろそろ30歳になります。

turn ～ ～歳になる

I'm turning 70 next year.

来年70歳になります。

in one's twenties 20歳代で

in one's early twenties 20歳代前半で

in one's mid-twenties	20歳代半ばで
in one's late twenties	20歳代後半で
an age bracket, an age range	年齢層
range in age from … to ～	…歳から～歳までの年齢の幅がある
the 20-29 age bracket	20歳から29歳の年齢層
the 60-80 age range	60歳から80歳の年齢層
people of that age	その年代の人
older than	よりも年が上
younger than	よりも年が下

I'm 45 years old.

私は45歳です。

She's 37 years of age.

彼女は37歳です。

My grandma is pushing eighty.

私の祖母はそろそろ80歳です。

Life begins at forty.

人生は40歳から始まる。

You can drink alcohol if you are 20 or older.

もし20歳以上であれば、アルコール飲料を飲める。

The photo contest is open to anyone 18 and up.

この写真コンテストは、18歳以上の人が参加できる。

or/and older, or/and over, and above, and up 〜歳以上

Eighty percent of the country's population are aged 40 or younger.

その国の人口の80％は40歳以下です。

or/and younger 〜歳以下

The average age of our employees is 28 years old.

弊社社員の平均年齢は28歳です。

average age　平均年齢

My daughter got married at the age of 32.

私の娘は32歳で結婚しました。

at the age of, at age, at　～歳で

His son started piano lessons from the age of five.

彼の息子は5歳からピアノのレッスンを始めました。

from the age of, from age　何歳から

My baby boy is three months old.

私の男の子の赤ん坊は生後3カ月です。

My three-month-old baby boy is still nursing.

私の生後3カ月の男の子はまだ授乳しています。

month-old　生後何月の

次の音声を聞き、空欄を埋めましょう。　)))Track 123

1. That tall tree is more than [　　　] years old.

2. My father has turned [　] today.

3. Our employees range in age from [　] to [　] years.

4. My son entered university at age [　　].

5. A: How much older is your husband?
   B: My husband is [　　] years older than I.

? | 問題 ▶ 空欄埋め

1. That tall tree is more than 1,000 years old.
2. My father has turned 57 today.
3. Our employees range in age from 18 to 65 years.
4. My son entered university at age 22.
5. A: How much older is your husband?

   B: My husband is three years older than I.

---

1. あの背の高い木は、樹齢が1,000年以上です。
2. 私の父親は今日、57歳になった。
3. 我が社の従業員の年齢層は18歳から65歳までです。
4. 私の息子は22歳で、大学に入学しました。
5. A：あなたのご主人は何歳年上ですか？

   B：私の主人は私より3歳年上です。

▶ 年、四半期、世代、月、週、日

年	»)) Track 124
half a year, a half year, six months	半年
a/one year	1年
a/one year and a half, one and a half years	1年半
two years, a couple of years	2年
ten years, one decade	10年
fifty years, half a century, a half century	50年
(one) hundred years, a/one century	100年、1世紀
a leap year	うるう年
annual, yearly	年一回の、毎年恒例の

四半期

quarterは4分の1を意味します。四半期は1年の4分の1なので、quarter
で表します。))) Track 125

a quarter	四半期
the first quarter	第1四半期
the second quarter	第2四半期
for the first time in seven quarters	7四半期ぶりに
in the second quarter of 2019	2019年の 第2四半期に
pay by the quarter	3カ月ごとに払う
a quarterly magazine	季刊雑誌

世代

1世代は約30年間で、生まれてから、成長して親になるまでの年数を表
します。))) Track 126

a/one generation	1世代
two generations	2世代
second generation	2代目
a first-generation immigrant to America	アメリカへの 移民の第1世

月

a/one month	1カ月
one and a half months, one month and a half	1カ月半
once a month	月に1度
twice a month	月に2度
several times a month	月に数回
a monthly magazine	月刊誌
monthly rent	1カ月の賃貸料

週

a/one week	1週間
three weeks' vacation	3週間の休暇
in the first week of December	12月の第1週
in the last week of January	1月の最後の週
for weeks	何週間もの間

twice a week	週に2回
a forty-hour week	週40時間労働

日

日に関する数、表現、イディオムは頻繁に使われるので、ぜひしっかり覚えて自分のものにしてください。日常会話でとても役立ちますよ。

))) Track 129

a/one day	1日
day one	1日目
half a day, a half day	半日
a day and a half, one and a half days	1日半
two days, a couple of days	2日間
one whole day	まる1日
all day	1日中
two days long	2日間の長さ
today	今日
yesterday	昨日

the day before yesterday	一昨日
tomorrow	明日
the day after tomorrow	明後日
three days ago	3日前
four days later	4日後
for the past few days	この数日間
the other day	先日
the previous day	その前の日
the last day of the week	その週の最終日
twice a day, twice daily	1日2度
three days a week	週に3日間
ten days a month	月に10日間
an eight-hour day	1日8時間労働
two days off	2日の休暇

☐ **This warranty is good for one year.**
この保証書は1年間有効です。

☐ **This is the worst typhoon in the past fifty years.**
これは、過去50年で最悪の台風です。

☐ **Our annual meeting is going to be held next week.**
来週わが社の年次会議が開催されます。

☐ **This clock has been in our family for four generations.**
この掛け時計は、私たちの家で4世代にわたって使われています。

☐ **The origins of the village fair go back many generations.**
その村の祭りの起源は、何世代も前にさかのぼります。

There are seven days in a week.

1週間は7日あります。

There are 365 days in a year.

1年は365日あります。

A leap year comes along every four years.

うるう年は、4年に1回あります。

Our plant workers are paid $180 per day.

私どもの工場労働者は1日に180ドルの賃金をもらっている。

We guarantee this product for three years.

この製品は3年間保証します。

I have 12 paid holidays this year.

今年の有給休暇は12日間あります。

次の音声を聞き、空欄を埋めましょう。　　))) **Track** 131

1. Our company is on a [　　　　　　] contract with that company.

2. I study Spanish [　　　　　　] a week.

3. She is [　　　　　　] pregnant.

4. I've lived in this town for [　　　　　].

5. I'm going to travel around Europe for [　　　　　　].

6. A：How long have you been married?
   B：We've been married for [　　　　　].

7. A：For how many generations has this business been in your family?

B：I'm the [   ] owner.

8. A：How many weeks are you planning to stay in Europe?

B：I'll stay in Europe for [   ].

9. A：How often do you play tennis a week?

B：[   ], on weekends.

10. A：When did you submit your monthly report?

B：I submitted my monthly report [   ] after the deadline.

06
▼
年、四半期、世代、月、週、日

(?) 問題 ▶ 空欄埋め

1. Our company is on a five-year contract with that company.
2. I study Spanish two days a week.
3. She is 13 weeks pregnant.
4. I've lived in this town for 15 years.
5. I'm going to travel around Europe for one and a half months.
6. A：How long have you been married?

   B：We've been married for 25 years.
7. A：For how many generations has this business been in your family?

   B：I'm the fifth-generation owner.
8. A：How many weeks are you planning to stay in Europe?

   B：I'll stay in Europe for three weeks.
9. A：How often do you play tennis a week?

   B：Twice a week, on weekends.
10. A：When did you submit your monthly report?

    B：I submitted my monthly report three days after the deadline.

1. 我が社はあの会社と5年契約を結んでいます。
2. 私は週に2日スペイン語を勉強します。
3. 彼女は妊娠13週目です。
4. 私はこの町に15年間住んでいます。
5. 1カ月半ヨーロッパを旅してまわります。
6. A：結婚してどのくらいたちますか？

   B：結婚して25年たちました。

7.　A：このビジネスはあなたの家で何代くらい続いているのですか？
　　B：私は5代目です。
8.　A：ヨーロッパには、何週間くらい滞在する予定ですか？
　　B：ヨーロッパには、3週間滞在します。
9.　A：週に何回テニスをしますか？
　　B：週に2回、週末に。
10.　A：あなたの月例報告書はいつ出しましたか？
　　B：締め切りの3日後に提出しました。

07 ▶時刻、時間、分、秒

時刻

Track 132

a.m./in the morning	午前、午前中
p.m./in the afternoon (evening)	午後
eight in the morning	午前8時
nine a.m.	午前9時
seven in the evening	午後7時
ten p.m.	午後10時
at noon	正午に
local time	現地時間

「○時○分」と言うとき、英語にはさまざまな表現があります。慣れていないと、なかなかすぐに理解できないので、しっかり身につけましょう。

まずは、数字をそのまま言う場合です。

Track 133

6:00 six o'clock

7:05　seven oh five

 zero ではなく oh といいます

8:24　eight twenty-four

past と to を使って表現する場合もあります。
30分（長い針が1〜6）までは past、30分以降（長い針が6〜12）は to
を使います。
past は○時から〜分経った、to は○時まで〜分という意味です。

))) Track 134

10:13　thirteen past ten

12:50　ten to one

また、30分は half、15分と45分は quarter という言い方をすることもあ
ります。

))) Track 135

11:15　a quarter past eleven

2:30　half past two

 half to three とはいいません

3:45　a quarter to four

時計を見たときには、心の中でもいいので英語でその時刻を言うように
習慣づけてみましょう。

時間)))Track 136

an/one hour	1時間
half an hour, a half hour	30分間、半時間
an hour's drive	車で1時間の距離
per/an hour	1時間当たり
wee/small/early hours	深夜過ぎ、未明、明け方前に
lunch/breakfast/dinner hour	昼食/朝食/夕食時間
visiting hours	訪問時間

分)))Track 137

a/one minute	1分
five minutes	5分
ten minutes	10分
fifteen minutes, a quarter of an hour	15分
thirty minutes, a half hour, half an hour	30分

forty-five minutes, three quarters of an hour	45分
sixty minutes	60分

秒

))) Track 138

one second	1秒
two seconds	2秒
one-tenth of a second	10分の1秒
one-hundredth of a second	100分の1秒
one-thousandth of a second	1000分の1秒
ten-thousandths of a second	1万分の1秒
one-hundred-thousandth of a second	10万分の1秒
one-millionth of a second	100万分の1秒
a 15-second TV commercial	15秒のテレビコマーシャル
one hour, fifty-six minutes, (and) forty-five seconds	1時間56分45秒

表現集

時刻を伝えるときはIt'sを使います。

☐ **It's ten (o'clock) in the morning.**
ただいま、朝の10時です。

☐ **It's eleven at night.**
ただいま午後11時です。

☐ **It's twelve midnight now.**
ただいま深夜12時です。

☐ **It has just struck seven.**
今ちょうど7時を打ったところです。

☐ **She set the alarm for five-thirty a.m.**
彼女は目覚まし時計を午前5時半にセットしました。

次の音声を聞き、空欄を埋めましょう。　　　》)) Track 140

1. It's [　　　　　　　].

2. I came home at [　　　　].

3. The meeting started at [　　　　　　　　].

4. It's [　　　] minutes to [　　　　　　　].

5. Let's take a [　　　]-minute break.

6. We'll have a [　　　]-minute lunch break at noon.

7. Bake the pizza for [　　　　　] minutes.

8. It's [　　　] minutes before [　　] in the morning.

9.
I was supposed to meet him at
[   ], but it's
already [   ].

10.
A : What's your local time now?
B : It's [   ]

(?) 問題 ▶ 空欄埋め

1. It's 7:23 a.m.
2. I came home at 5:16.
3. The meeting started at half past ten.
4. It's five minutes to seven p.m.
5. Let's take a five-minute break.
6. We'll have a 45-minute lunch break at noon.
7. Bake the pizza for twelve minutes.
8. It's ten minutes before six in the morning.
9. I was supposed to meet him at quarter past eight, but it's already ten to nine.
10. A : What's your local time now?
    B : It's ten at night.

1. 午前7：23です。
2. 5：16に家に帰ってきました。
3. 会議は10：30に始まりました。
4. 午後7時5分前です。
5. 5分間休憩しましょう。
6. 私たちはお昼に45分間の休憩を取ります。
7. ピザを12分間焼きなさい。
8. 午前の6時10分前です。
9. 彼に8：15に会うはずだったんですが、もう8：50です。
10. A：そちらの現地時間は何時ですか？
    B：夜の10時です。

時計

私は時計を集めるのが趣味で、約60個所有しています。Rolex社の時計は自動巻（automatic）が人気があり、デイトナというステンレスのモデルでも300万円近くします。また、自動巻は年数がたつと値上がりするものが多くあります。一方、Rolexのクオーツ時計に人気がなく、値上がりしません。

ひと言に「時計」といっても、種類によって英語での呼び方はさまざまです。区別して使えるようになりましょう。あわせて、時計に関する表現もご紹介します。

watch/wristwatch	腕時計
pocket watch	懐中時計
clock	掛け時計
egg timer	卵用タイマー
alarm clock	目覚まし時計
stopwatch	ストップウオッチ
hour hand	時針
minute hand	分針
second hand	秒針
mineral glass	ミネラルガラス
sapphire glass	サファイアガラス
gold plated	金メッキ

solid gold	金無垢
automatic	自動巻
quartz	クオーツ
solar	ソーラー発電
gain	進む
lose	遅れる
strike	時刻を打つ
fast	進んでいる
slow	遅れている

■ Our clock strikes every hour.

家の掛け時計は毎時間鳴ります。

■ My watch is automatic/self-winding.

私の時計は自動巻です。

 ⇔ battery-operated 電池式

■ His watch loses one minute per day.

彼の時計は1日に1分遅れます。

■ That clock is five minutes fast.

あの掛け時計は5分進んでいます。

08

▶ 天気、温度

日本やイギリスでは摂氏 Celsius/centigrade を、アメリカでは華氏 Fahrenheit を使っています。従って、アメリカで華氏の天気予報を聞いた場合には、それを摂氏になおして理解する必要があります。それを行う数式もありますが、大体の換算表を知っていた方が役立つので、ご紹介します。

華氏の温度	摂氏の温度
0°F	-18°C
20°F	-7°C
32°F	0°C
50°F	10°C
68°F	20°C
87°F	31°C
100°F	38°C

There is an 80% chance of rain.

雨の降る確率は80％でしょう。

Last night the temperature fell below freezing.

昨晩、気温が零度以下に下がった。

Please raise the room temperature by 3 degrees.

部屋の温度を3度上げてください。

The temperature rose to 37 degrees Celsius yesterday.

昨日、気温が摂氏37度まで上昇した。

Today's high is expected to be in the high eighties.

今日の最高気温は、（華氏）80度台後半が予想されています。

 ⇔ in the low 最低気温

☐ **There is a 50 percent chance of precipitation tomorrow.**

明日の降水確率は50％でしょう。

☐ **Some hard-core golfers play in sub-zero temperatures.**

ゴルフ大好きな人の中には、零度以下の温度でもプレーする人もいます。

☐ **A：How warm is it?**

B：It's 23 degrees Celsius.

A：（暖かい日に）何度ですか？
B：摂氏23度です。

☐ **A：How cold is it?**

B：It's two degrees below zero.

A：（寒い日に）何度ですか？
B：零下2度です。

次の音声を聞き、空欄を埋めましょう。　　　))) Track 142

1. The temperature fell to
   [   ] last night.

2. The thermometer reads [   ]
   Celsius now.

3. We keep the temperature in this room at
   [   ] Celsius.

4. Tomorrow's high will be [   ]
   Celsius, and the low, [   ]
   Celsius.

5. Tomorrow's low is forecast to be in the
   [   ].

6. [   ] Celsius equals
   [   ] Fahrenheit.

A: How hot is it?

7.   B: The current temperature is close to
[   ] Celsius.

A: What's the weather forecast for tomorrow?

8.   B: There is a [   ]. You had better take an umbrella.

1. The temperature fell to minus twelve last night.
2. The thermometer reads 28 degrees Celsius now.
3. We keep the temperature in this room at 25 degrees Celsius.
4. Tomorrow's high will be 33 degrees Celsius, and the low, 23 degrees Celsius.
5. Tomorrow's low is forecast to be in the low sixties.
6. Ten degrees Celsius equals 50 degrees Fahrenheit.
7. A: How hot is it?
   B: The current temperature is close to 38 degrees Celsius.
8. A: What's the weather forecast for tomorrow?
   B: There is a 50% chance of rain. You had better take an umbrella.

1. 昨晩、気温が零下12度まで下がった。
2. 現在、温度計は摂氏28度を指している。
3. 私たちはこの部屋の温度を摂氏25度に保っている。
4. 明日の最高気温は摂氏33度、最低気温は摂氏23度でしょう。
5. 明日の最低気温は、華氏60度台の前半の温度が予想されています。
6. 摂氏10度は華氏の50度に相当する。
7. A：（暑い日に）何度ですか？
   B：現在の気温は38度近くあります。
8. A：明日の天気予報はどうですか？
   B：雨が降る確率が50％あります。傘を持って行ったほうがいいですよ。

09 ▶ 回数、頻度

回数や頻度を表す言葉で頻繁に使われるのがonce, twice です。「3回」は thrice という言葉がありますが、旧式で、現在ではほとんど使われていません。その代わり、three times が使われます。))) Track 143

1回	once/one time only
2回	twice/two times, a couple of times
3回	three times/thrice（旧式な言い方）
4回	four times
5回	five times
6回	six times
7回	seven times
8回	eight times
9回	nine times
10回	ten times
何百回も	hundreds of times

何千回も	thousands of times
数えられない くらい何度も	countless times
数回	a few times/several times
何回も	many times
何回も何回も	many, many times
複数回	multiple times
回数	the number of times

何回目	))) Track 144
1回目	first time
2回目	second time
3回目	third time
4回目	fourth time
5回目	fifth time
6回目	sixth time

7回目	seventh time
8回目	eighth time
9回目	ninth time
10回目	tenth time

CHAPTER 3 ▼ 数字を使って伝える

))) Track 145

I met her for the first time 20 years ago.

私が彼女に最初にあったのは20年前でした。

This is my third time to visit Japan.

これは私の3回目の日本訪問です。

The second time I visited his office, he was out on business.

2度目に私が彼の事務所に訪ねると、彼は仕事で外出していた。

The 29th of February only comes once every four years.

2月29日は、4年に一度しかやって来ません。

We visited them six times last year.

私たちは彼らを昨年6回訪問しました。

How many times a day do you brush your teeth?

1日に何回歯を磨きますか？

問題 1 ▶ 書き取り　　　　　　　　　　解答は226ページ

次の日本語を英語で書きましょう。

....

1.　2度目

....

2.　何度も何度も

....

3.　何百回も

....

4.　5回目

....

5.　数え切れないほど何度も

....

CHAPTER 3 ▼ 数字を使って伝える

次の音声を聞き、空欄を埋めましょう。　　　))) **Track** 146

1. A：How many times have you been to the States?

   B：I've been there [　　　　　　　].

2. A：How often do you go to the movies a month?

   B：I go to the movies [　　　　　] or
   [　　　　　　　　　　　].

3. A：How often is the mail delivered a week on this
   island?

   B：The mail is delivered here
   [　　　　　　　　　　　　　].

4. A：How often do you go to the bathroom a day?

   B：During the daytime, I go about
   [　　　　　　].

5. A：How many times have you taken the National
   Bar Examination?

   B：This is my [　　　　　　　] time.

▶ 解答・日本語訳

問題 1 ▶ 書き取り

1. second time
2. many, many times
3. hundreds of times
4. fifth time
5. countless times

問題 2 ▶ 空欄埋め

1. A：How many times have you been to the States?
   B：I've been there five times.
2. A：How often do you go to the movies a month?
   B：I go to the movies once or twice a month.
3. A：How often is the mail delivered a week on this island?
   B：The mail is delivered here three times a week.
4. A：How often do you go to the bathroom a day?
   B：During the daytime, I go about six times.
5. A：How many times have you taken the National Bar Examination?
   B：This is my seventh time.

1. A：アメリカへは今までに何度行きましたか？
   B：5回行きました。
2. A：1カ月に何回くらい映画に行きますか？
   B：月に1度か2度、映画に行きます。

CHAPTER 3 ▼ 数字を使って伝える

3. A：この島では、1週間に何度、郵便が配達されますか？
   B：ここでは郵便は週に3回配達されます。
4. A：1日に何回くらいトイレに行きますか？
   B：昼間に6回くらいトイレに行きます。
5. A：今までに何回司法試験を受けましたか？
   B：これが7度目の試験です。

10 ▶ 重さ、体重

日本と英米では、重さの単位が違います。グラムやキログラムではなく、ポンドやオンスを使うのが主流です。)))) Track 147

one gram	1グラム
one kilogram	1キログラム
two kilograms	2キログラム
one pound	1ポンド
one and a half pounds	1.5ポンド
two pounds	2ポンド
one ounce	1オンス

One pound equals 16 ounces.

1ポンドは16オンスに相当します。

one stone	1ストーン（14ポンド相当）
one ton	1トン
weight	重さ

weight of 5 kg	5キロの重さ
dead weight	載貨重量・積載重量

対応表

1 milligram (mg) = 0.015 grain

10 milligrams = 0.154 grain

1 decigram (dm) = 1.543 grains

1 gram (g) = 15.43 grains

10 grams = 5.64 drams

100 grams = 3.527 ounces

1 kilogram (kg) = 2.205 pounds

1 ton (metric ton) = 0.984 (long) ton

換算表

Metric	Multiply by	To get standard
grams	0.035	ounces
kilograms	2.2	pounds
metric tons	1.1	short tons

weighやweightを使った、さまざまな重さの伝え方の表現があります。

))) Track 148

☐ **The letter weighs 5 grams.**

手紙は5グラムの重さがある。

📖 weigh 重さを量る、重さがある

☐ **The gross weight is 72 grams.**

総重量は72グラムです。

📖 gross weight 総重量

☐ **The net weight is 60 grams.**

正味重量は60グラムです。

📖 net weight 正味重量

☐ **His opinion carries weight.**

彼の意見は影響力を持っている。

☐ **He spoke calmly, but each sentence carried weight.**

彼は静かに話したが、一文ごとに重みがあった。

📖 carry weight 影響力がある

I weigh 12 stone.

私は体重が12ストーン（約76キロ）です。

※ one stone は6.35キロの重さがあり、イギリスでは、この言い方をする人がいます。

weigh 体重がある、weight 体重

I gained ten pounds in six months.

私は6カ月で10ポンド体重が増えました。

gain weight/put on weight 体重が増える

I have to lose weight.

私は体重を減らさなければなりません。

lose weight 体重が減る

You're a great asset to our company. You're worth your weight in gold.

あなたは会社にとって重要な財産です。とても会社に貢献しています。

worth one's weight in gold とても役立つ
自分の体重に相当する金ほどの価値がある、が元の意味。

次の音声を聞き、空欄を埋めましょう。　))) Track 149

1. Your bag weighs [　　　　　].

2. I'll buy [　　　　　　　] of roast beef.

3. I would like to buy [　　　　　　　] of scallops.

4. The gross weight is [　　　　　　　].

5. A：I weigh [　　　　　].
   B：You had better **go on a diet**.

📖 go on a diet　ダイエットする

233

10
▼
重
さ
、
体
重

? 問題 ▶ 空欄埋め

1. Your bag weighs 20 kg.
2. I'll buy a pound of roast beef.
3. I would like to buy eight ounces of scallops.
4. The gross weight is 13 pounds.
5. A:I weigh 15 stone.

   B:You had better go on a diet.

1. あなたのかばんは20キロです。
2. ロースト・ビーフを1ポンド買いたいです。
3. 貝柱を8オンス買いたいです。
4. 総重量は13ポンドです。
5. A：体重は15ストーンです。

   B：ダイエットした方がいいですよ。

11

▶ 長さ、幅、高さ、身長

ヤード・ポンド法とメートル法

アメリカでは、完全にメートル法には移行していません。しかし、世界の95%の国がメートル法を採用しているので、貿易の面から不利だと理解しています。科学と医学の分野ではメートル法のみを使っています。距離（mile）、長さ（feet）、重さ（pound）では、ヤード・ポンド法が正式に認められています。また、いつ全面的にメートル法になるのかも決定されていません。

イギリスでも1965年に一度はメートル法が採択されましたが、1980年にはそれが反故になりました。距離、速度、液体ではメートル法が公式になっています。しかし現在でも、統計（2011）によると70%の人は「メートル法は混乱をまねく」と答えています。全面的なメートル法への移行の時期は決定されていません。

長さ   ))) Track 150

a/one millimeter	1ミリメートル

One millimeter equals one-thousandth of a meter.

1ミリメートルは、千分の1メートルです。

a/one centimeter	1センチメートル
a/one meter	1メートル

a/one kilometer	1キロメートル
one point five meters	1.5メートル
two kilometers	2キロメートル
six point two three kilometers	6.23 キロメートル
an/one inch	1インチ
a quarter of an inch	4分の1インチ
a/one foot	1フィート
two feet	2フィート
a/one yard	1ヤード
three yards	3ヤード
a/one mile	1マイル

One mile equals 1.6 kilometers.

1マイルは1.6キロに相当します。

half a/a half mile	2分の1マイル

a nautical mile	海里

One nautical mile equals 1,852 meters.

1海里は、1,852メートルに相当します。

length	長さ

幅　　　　　　　　　　　　　　　　　　　))) Track 151

width	幅
wide	幅がある
a strip of tape 5 cm wide	幅5センチのテープ

高さ、身長　　　　　　　　　　　　　　))) Track 152

height, altitude	高さ、標高
high, tall	高い、背がある

対応表

1 millimeter (mm) = 0.039 inch

1 centimeter (cm) = 0.394 inch

10 centimeters = 3.94 inches

1 meter (m) = 1.094 yards

10 meters = 10.94 yards

100 meters = 109.4 yards

1 kilometer (km) = 0.6214 mile

CHAPTER 3 ▼ 数字を使って伝える

換算表

Metric	Multiply by	To get standard
millimeters	0.04	inches
centimeters	0.4	inches
meters	3.3	feet
meters	1.1	yards
kilometers	0.6	miles

))) Track 153

☐ **This swimming pool is 25 meters long.**
このプールは25メートルの長さです。

☐ **Our English lesson is 90 minutes long/in length.**
私たちの英語の授業は90分の長さです。

☐ **This book is 780 pages long.**
この本は780頁あります。

☐ **One block in Manhattan is 80 meters wide and 274 meters long.**
マンハッタンの1ブロックは、幅が80メートルで、長さが274メートルあります。

☐ **This table is eight feet wide.**
このテーブルは幅が8フィートある。

 eight feet in width という表現もあります。

I need a wider notebook than this one.

私はこれよりももっと幅の広いノートが必要です。

This river is the widest in the country.

この川は国の中で一番川幅が広い。

I could see that my manager was in a bad mood, so I gave him a wide berth.

私は、上司の機嫌が悪いことが分かったので、近づかないようにした。

My wife is 5 feet, 5 inches tall.

私の妻は背が5フィート5インチあります。

Tom is the tallest student in our class.

トムは私たちのクラスで一番背が高い。

次の音声を聞き、空欄を埋めましょう。　　　))) Track 154

1.
A：What is the length of the bridge?

B：It is [　　　　　　　　　　　　　　].

2.
A：What's the width of the table?

B：It's [　　　　　　　　　　　].

3.
A：What's the height of the building?

B：It's [　　　　　　　　　　　].

4.
A：How high is Mount Fuji?

B：It's [　　　　　　　　　　　].

5.
A：How wide is the river at the widest part?

B：It is [　　　　　　　] wide at the widest part.

(?) 問題 ▶ 空欄埋め

1. A：What is the length of the bridge?
   B：It is 1,796 meters long.
2. A：What's the width of the table?
   B：It's 1.5 meters wide.
3. A：What's the height of the building?
   B：It's 210 meters high.
4. A：How high is Mount Fuji?
   B：It's 3,776 meters high.
5. A：How wide is the river at the widest part?
   B：It is 75 yards wide at the widest part.

1. A：その橋の長さはどのくらいありますか？
   B：1,796メートルの長さです。
2. A：テーブルの幅はどのくらいですか？
   B：幅は1.5メートルあります。
3. A：そのビルの高さはどのくらいですか？
   B：210メートルの高さがあります。
4. A：富士山はどのくらいの高さですか？
   B：3,776メートルの高さがあります。
5. A：その川は、一番川幅の広い場所でどのくらいの幅がありますか？
   B：一番広い場所で、75ヤードあります。

エンパイア・ステートビルの話

私はニューヨークに赴任していたときに、数回、マンハッタンにそびえ立つEmpire State Buildingに登ったことがあります。周辺には、韓国系の惣菜店やレストランがたくさんあります。このビルは、1929年の大恐慌から景気を立て直すために建設が行われ1931年に完成し、当時では世界一高いビルでした。この記録は1972年まで続きました。高さが443.2メートルもあります。建設後しばらくは、借りる会社が少なくて、空いている部屋や階が多く、Empty State Buildingという不名誉なあだ名で呼ばれたこともありました。

私が登ったのは102階にある展望台で、そこでも、高さが381メートルあります。エレベーターを乗り継いでその展望台に降りると、その階全体が、左右に数メートル揺れていました。日本から来た同僚を連れて行ったのですが、彼はとても恐がりで、近くにあった柱にかじりつき、浅見さん、早く、降りましょうよ、と青くなって私に訴えてきました。私は、怖いことが大好きなので、床の揺れを楽しんでいましたが、彼のことがかわいそうになったので、仕方なくエレベーターに乗って下に降りました。ちょうどその日は、ビルから飛び降りた自殺者がいたので、ビル周辺には、パトカーや救急車がたくさんいました。エンパイア・ステートビルから自殺しようとして飛び降りた人は、今までに30名以上いるそうですが、助かったのは2人だけで、2人とも86階の展望台から飛び降りて、横風に吹かれて、85階の棚状の突起の上に着地して命拾いをしたそうです。

1978年からは、毎年恒例のEmpire State Building Run-Upが開催されています。地上階から86階までの320メートルの高さと、1,576段を駆け上がった記録保持者は、オーストラリア人のサイクリストで9分33秒しかかからなかったそうです。ちなみに、かつては尖塔部分が飛行船を係留できるようになっていたそうです。

読者の皆様もマンハッタンへ行く機会がありましたら、是非ともEmpire State Buildingに登ってみてください。

CHAPTER

4

· ·

チャレンジ問題

次の音声を聞き、空欄を埋めましょう。　　))) Track 155

1. My wife makes ¥[　　　　　　　] a day as a tour guide.

2. Tokyo Tower is [　　　　] meters high.

3. It's [　　　　　　　　　　　　　　　　　] in the morning.

CHAPTER 4 ▼ チャレンジ問題

4. My granddaughter grew [　　　　　] centimeters in one year.

5. Your rent is nearly [　　　　　] days overdue.

6. I weigh [　　　] kilos.

7. This plane is flying at an altitude of [　　　　　] meters.

A: How often do you visit Hawaii?

8.
B: I visit there [   ] every [   ] years.
One of my friends has been living in Hawaii since
[   ].

A: We'd like to have [   ] tables for
[   ] of us.

B: Sorry, but we have [   ] table for
9.
[   ] people and [   ] tables for
[   ] people each.

A: That's fine. We'll take them.

A: How many [   ] GB SD cards are there in
your stock?

10.
B: Let me check. We have a total of [   ] cards.

A: I'll take all of them. Do you offer any discount?

B: We'll take [   ] % off the list price.

11.
A：What's the population of Yokohama?

B：As of [   ], it has an
estimated population of about
[   ].

12.
A：How many Japanese cars were exported to the
U.S.A. per year?

B：In [   ], about [   ]
Japanese cars were exported to the U.S.A.

13.
A：What are the populations of Japan and the
U.S.A.?

B：As of [   ], Japan has a population of
about [   ], and the U.S.A.
has [   ].

A：That means the U.S.A. has more than
[   ] as many people as Japan.

B：You're exactly right.

A:Do you have the time?

B:It's [   ].

14.

A:When will Mr. Smith come?

B:I guess he'll come in [   ].

A:When was your company founded?

B:Our company was founded [   ].

A:What month is the busiest for your business?

15.

B:December is the busiest.

A:Where does your company rank in the industry?

B:We rank [   ].

A:Thank you for calling. How may I help you?

B:I'd like to book a table for [   ] at [   ] tonight.

A:I'm afraid it's already full at [   ].

16. B:How about [   ] o'clock?

A:That's fine. May I have your name and phone number, please?

B:My last name is Yamada, and my number is

[   ].

? 問題 ▶ 空欄埋め

1. My wife makes ¥25,000 a day as a tour guide.

2. Tokyo Tower is 333 meters high.

3. It's ten minutes before nine in the morning.

4. My granddaughter grew eight centimeters in one year.

5. Your rent is nearly twenty days overdue.

6. I weigh 75 kilos.

7. This plane is flying at an altitude of 12,000 meters.

8. A: How often do you visit Hawaii?

   B: I visit there once every four years. One of my friends has been living in Hawaii since 2005.

9. A: We'd like to have two tables for eight of us.

   B: Sorry, but we have one table for four people and two tables for two people each.

   A: That's fine. We'll take them.

10. A: How many 128 GB SD cards are there in your stock?

    B: Let me check. We have a total of 12 cards.

    A: I'll take all of them. Do you offer any discount?

    B: We'll take 10% off the list price.

11. A: What's the population of Yokohama?

    B: As of June 1st, 2019, it has an estimated population of about 3.75 million.

12. A: How many Japanese cars were exported to the U.S.A. per year?

    B: In 2018, about 1.7 million Japanese cars were exported to the

U.S.A.

13. A: What are the populations of Japan and the U.S.A.?

B: As of 2018, Japan has a population of about 126 million, and the U.S.A. has 327 million.

A: That means the U.S.A. has more than twice as many people as Japan.

B: You're exactly right.

14. A: Do you have the time?

B: It's half past two.

A: When will Mr. Smith come?

B: I guess he'll come in ten minutes.

15. A: When was your company founded?

B: Our company was founded in 1926.

A: What month is the busiest for your business?

B: December is the busiest.

A: Where does your company rank in the industry?

B: We rank third.

16. A: Thank you for calling. How may I help you?

B: I'd like to book a table for four at six tonight.

A: I'm afraid it's already full at six.

B: How about seven o'clock?

A: That's fine. May I have your name and phone number please?

B: My last name is Yamada, and my number is 080-1256-3478.

----

1. 私の妻はツアーガイドとして、1日に2万5千円稼ぎます。

2. 東京タワーは高さが333メートルあります。

3. 午前の9時10分前です。

4. 私の孫娘は、1年間で8センチ背が伸びました。

5. あなたの家賃の支払いは、ほぼ20日間過ぎていますよ。

6. 私は体重が75キロです。

7. 当機は、高度1万2千メートルを飛行しています。

8. A：どれくらいの頻度でハワイを訪れていますか？

   B：4年に一度、訪れています。友人の一人が2005年からハワイに住んでいるんです。

9. A：我々8人で2つのテーブルをお願いしたいのですが。

   B：申し訳ありませんが、4名様用のテーブルが1つと、2名様用のテーブルが2つしかありません。

   A：それでいいです。お願いします。

10. A：そちらのストックに何枚の128 GBのSDカードがありますか？

    B：ちょっと調べてみます。全部で12枚あります。

    A：全部お願いします。割引はしていただけるのですか？

    B：定価から10％引かせていただきます。

11. A：横浜市の人口は何人ですか？

    B：2019年6月1日現在で、予想人口は約375万人です。

12. A：年間何台の日本車がアメリカに輸出されていますか？

    B：2018年に、約170万台の日本車がアメリカに輸出されました。

13. A：日本と米国の人口はどのくらいですか？

    B：2018年現在で、日本の人口は1億2,600万人で、アメリカは3億2,700万人です。

    A：そうすると、アメリカには、日本の2倍以上の人口がいるということですね。

    B：全くあなたの言う通りです。

14. A：今何時ですか？

B：2時半です。

A：スミスさんはいつきますか？

B：10分以内にはくると思います。

15. A：御社はいつ設立されたのですか？

B：我が社は1926年に設立されました。

A：あなたの仕事の繁忙期は何月ですか？

B：12月が一番忙しいです。

A：御社は業界で何位に位置しますか？

B：我々は3位にランクしています。

16. A：お電話ありがとうございます。ご用件をお伺いします。

B：今晩6時に4名で予約をしたいのですが。

A：申し訳ございません、6時はすでに満席となっております。

B：7時はどうですか？

A：それなら問題ありません。お名前とお電話番号をお願いします。

B：ラストネームは山田です。番号は080-1256-3478です。

自分のことを伝えられるようになろう！

ここまでいろいろな数字を学習してきましたが、自分に関する数字は言えますか？仕事でもプライベートでも、自分や自分の会社のことを伝える機会はたくさんあります。焦らずしっかり伝えられるように準備しておきましょう。

■ **My birthday is 〜.**
私の誕生日は〜です。

■ **I was born in 〜.**
〜年に生まれました。

■ **I joined this company in 〜.**
〜年に入社しました。

■ **Our company was established in 〜.**
弊社は〜年に設立しました。

■ **My phone number is 〜.**
私の電話番号は〜です。

いつでもパッと言えるように、くり返し練習しておきましょう。

浅見ベートーベン　本名：浅見ベートーベン・スミス

英語研修サービス有限会社社長、長野県の軽井沢で、アメリカ人の父親と日本人の母親の間に1947年に生まれる。1歳から、東京の赤羽で育つ。日本IBMと筑波大学大学院博士課程でビジネス英語を教える。NHKラジオテキスト「入門ビジネス英語」の執筆を含め、著書は50冊を超え、Kindleのe-bookでの出版も30冊以上ある。明治大学商学部とコーネル大学で鳥類学を学ぶ、ジョージア大学でマーケット・リサーチャーのプロ資格を得る、35年間日本IBMに勤務し、その間、合計で6年間IBMのニューヨーク本社で勤務、アジア・パシフィック本社にてプロダクト・マネジャーにつく。日本IBMでは、2000名以上の社員に、英語によるプレゼン、交渉術、ビジネスレターの書き方、電話会議、TOEICの高得点獲得法、速読術等を教えてきた。日本IBMの全教員のなかで、生徒の評価で第1位を獲得。資格としては、TOEIC連続満点（990点）取得、英検1級、ガイドの国家試験（英語）、ビジネス英検Grade Aなどに合格。

主な著書としては：

「ビジネスパーソンのための英語イディオム辞典」（NHK出版）、「ビジネス英語の敬語」（クロスメディア・ランゲージ）、「ビジネス英語フレーズブック」（明日香出版社）、「2週間で英語の読解スピードが3倍になる本」（アスク出版）、「最新必須英文法」（IBCパブリッシング）他多数

趣味は：

50年以上続けるBirdwatchingと野鳥写真撮影、柔道4段、文房具収集、読書（主に英語）、カラオケ、食べ歩き、ダジャレ

肉体的特徴：

西郷隆盛と身長体重が同じ、179cm、115キロ、外見はほぼアメリカ人

家族：

妻と男子2人、孫が3人

瞬時に「わかる」！
数字の英語

2020年 4月27日　初版　第1刷発行

著者	浅見 ベートーベン
発行者	天谷 修平
発行	株式会社オープンゲート
	〒101-0051　東京都千代田区神保町2-14　SP神保町ビル5階
	TEL：03-5213-4125　FAX：03-5213-4126
印刷・製本	株式会社 光邦
装丁デザイン	大野 真琴（株式会社 鷗来堂）
本文デザイン	大野 真琴（株式会社 鷗来堂）
DTP	株式会社 鷗来堂
録音・編集	ユニバ合同会社
ナレーション	Josh Keller, Jenny Skidmore

ISBN 978-4-9910999-8-4